THEATRE

Desmond MacCarthy

THEATRE

GREENWOOD PRESS, PUBLISHERS
WESTPORT, CONNECTICUT

Library of Congress Cataloging in Publication Data

MacCarthy, Desmond, Sir, 1878-1952.
   Theatre.

    Reprint of the 1954 ed. published by MacGibbon & Kee,
London.
    1. Theater--England--London--Reviews. 2. Drama--
History and criticism--Addresses, essays, lectures.
I. Title.
[PN2596.16M25 1976]   792'.01   76-49881
ISBN 0-8371-9333-8

ACKNOWLEDGEMENTS

The publishers' grateful thanks are due to the following for help or permission to reprint essays in this book : Lord David Cecil and Mr Michael MacCarthy for their assistance in choosing the essays, many of which were included by Messrs Putnam & Co. Ltd. in *Drama,* now out of print; 'Good Talk' was published by the same firm in *Experience,* also out of print; nearly all the criticisms of actual productions were first published in *The New Statesman* when Sir Desmond MacCarthy was their dramatic critic; the first six essays on Modern Drama were broadcast talks traced with the assistance of the B.B.C. Librarian and the essay on 'Censorship' was a lecture given in 1929 when the subject was as topical as it has become again today.

Originally published in 1954 by MacGibbon & Kee, London

Reprinted with the permission of The Trustees of Michael D. MacCarthy

Reprinted in 1976 by Greenwood Press, Inc.

Library of Congress Catalog Card Number 76-49881

ISBN 0-8371-9333-8

Printed in the United States of America

CONTENTS

MODERN DRAMA

SHAKESPEARE

CONTINENTAL DRAMATISTS

67699

ENGLISH PLAYS

PLAYERS

TWO ESSAYS

MODERN DRAMA

MODERN DRAMA

THE IDEAL SPECTATOR

1930

I HAVE BEEN A dramatic critic (on and off) for over twenty-five years. I have had therefore to attend to the drama and make myself as far as possible into an ideal spectator. Who then is the Ideal Spectator? Well, of course, he must be one who is naturally preoccupied with human nature, since human nature is the stuff out of which drama is made. In the second place he must grasp the peculiar advantages and limitations which stage representation imposes on the treatment of any subject. And lastly, he must (this applies, however, equally to the critic of literature) take into account the aim in any particular case of the dramatist, not only in relation to his subject but in relation to his audience. What the phrase 'in relation to his audience' means may not be at once clear. What it means is that it is not only unfair to a play, but also silly from the point of view of our own pleasure to ask from it something which its author never intended it to provide. It is silly, for example, to crab your own enjoyment of a comedy, say, like *The Farmer's Wife*, because it is intended merely to amuse. The genuine dramatic critic is the spectator who gets most out of a play even if at the same time he notices its shortcomings, and the ideal audience is therefore an audience of dramatic critics. Now it may possibly help you to get all you can out of the theatre to describe briefly my own experience as a professional critic. Dramatic critics, owing to the various nature of the works upon which they must pronounce, learn, like very agreeable people of too wide acquaintance, to develop their multiple personalities. The same man no doubt writes the articles, but the same critic does not always attend the plays. In my case, D. M. No. 1, who is not easy to satisfy, and thinks nearly every play produced throughout the year practically negligible from the point of view of art (What else could he expect ? Do masterpieces cluster every year ?), seldom puts his nose into a theatre, or, if he does, the first act, like a mesmeric pass, puts him asleep, and leaves D. M. No. 2 in control. He is, as a rule, a much more serviceable, generally useful, critic. The faculties of No. 1 need only be requisitioned when something exceptional comes along, or a cry of 'Lo Here!' arises over nothing in particular.

D. M. No. 2 has a natural taste for the theatre; the drop curtain fills him with agreeable expectations; he cries and laughs easily; a little common sense in a dramatist enraptures him; he feels all the time that it is very good of the management and actors to have taken such pains to get everything shipshape; he has never been able to understand how people can begin fishing for their hats during the last five minutes of any play. He forgets there are such things as masterpieces; he really thinks (though it sounds stupid to say so) the author very clever to have written a play at all; though ways in which it might be improved may keep occurring to him, his comments are mostly made from the point of view of truth. 'Do I believe in these people ? Why do they or don't they interest me ?' Such is D. M. No. 2. Of course, the stage being what it is, the bulk of the work falls upon this good-natured and impressionable creature, and I have had all my life to make the best of such reports as he sends me. Now I expect nearly every thorough playgoer is conscious of two such critics in himself. There is, too, a D. M. No. 3, but I will not bore you with him.

Now sometimes it happens that the play is of such as kind that though D. M. No. 1 says, 'This is your job, No. 2', he cannot get off to sleep; he is kept awake either because there is a broken, frustrated, poetic force running through the play, or because it flies ambitiously high in its aim. And when No. 1 cannot efface himself and yet keeps grumbling, while No. 2 goes on picking holes from the point of view of matters of fact, the result must be an unfavourable notice.

Now, whether you recognise yourselves or not in this description, it contains a hint for you. If you judge every play from the point of view of that self which is only gratified by what is really excellent and significant, and without exaggeration can claim to be a work of art, then you will not only be very dissatisfied play-goers but unintelligent ones. The mind of the ideal spectator must, like a good motor-car, run on several gears; and from different plays you must ask not only different experiences, but be content with different qualities of enjoyment, sometimes with trivial ones.

But is there anything which you can demand from every play? I think there is: something must happen. The stage is particularly fitted to exhibit action. You can be immensely interested by a discussion on the stage as you might be in a debating hall or listening to the wireless, but since one of the essential advantages of the drama in contrast to all other forms is that you can *see*, with a vividness no description, however masterly, can achieve, something actually happening, not to use that advantage is to neglect the peculiar virtue of your medium. You can produce a highly instructive end enthralling entertainment without doing so—Mr Shaw has done it again and again—and one which is more worth attending than many plays which do exhibit something happening, but such a work can never rank among the world's first-rate plays. The best drama is that which incorporates its idea in action as well as in dialogue. Take Ibsen's *The Wild Duck*, for example. The theme of the wild duck—it is a tragic comedy, and this is the form of tragedy most acceptable to the modern mind—is that there are such things as vital lies, or illusions. In that play Ibsen faced the fact that it is not necessarily truth that saves men, that truth may, indeed, destroy them. *The Wild Duck* must have astonished his disciples when it first appeared; it looked like a satire on his own philosophy. It was an assult on 'Ibsenites', on men and women who think that to blurt out the truth, and destroy everything which has an alloy of compromise and sham in it, is the remedy for social and private evils. Nothing Ibsen has written makes us respect him more.

He has always declared that, 'What is wanted is a revolution in the spirit of man'; in this play he faces the reformer's worst trial, recognition of the fundamental weakness of human nature. We are shown a group of dilapidated creatures, each of whom, maimed by life, has dived beneath its surface, as the wild duck dives after it has been mortally wounded. It is perhaps the most perfectly constructed of all Ibsen's plays. The idea of the play is audible when Relling, a rough, damaged, disappointed fellow himself, says that 'life would be quite tolerable if only we could get rid of the confounded duns that keep on pestering us in our poverty with the claims of the ideal' and that 'when a man has no hair of his own he must wear a wig, that is, find shelter for that necessary minimum of self-respect in some consoling illusion.' In the play the catastrophe is brought about, and the theme itself expressed, by the tragic results of the well-meaning interference of a busy-body idealist. A terrible thing happens. It is a theme which would have also lent itself admirably to a stage discussion. The tipsy broken old hunter in the play could have expatiated on the happiness he found in shooting rabbits in a garret; the ridiculous Hialmer upon all that his 'invention' meant to him, and the protagonists, the realist Relling and the idealist Gregers, might in a hammer-and-tongs argument, ranging up and down the whole of experience, have thrashed out for us in the most exhilarating way the value of truth to humanity. Such a treatment of the theme might produce a stimulating entertainment, clarifying the minds of all who heard it, but, whatever its merits, it would be one which failed to take full advantage of the emphasis which the stage alone can supply. The triumph of the dramatist is to take advantage of this and to embody his idea in a story completely, as a sculptor expresses it in stone or bronze. Failing that, he may excite and instruct us through the clash of ideas and points of view—a great service, but one of less impressiveness than if he had incorporated those ideas in events.

If you examine the discussion plays of Bernard Shaw, *Getting Married*, *Misalliance*, *The Apple Cart* you will notice that although the author has hardly attempted to do this, he has used to some extent the peculiar virtue of stage-representation. He has introduced events, which only aid discussion in an ancillary way: the crash of an aeroplane in *Misalliance*; in *Getting Married* the doubt—Will a particular marriage after all take place?; and in *The Apple Cart* again suspense—Will the king get the better of his ministers? Although Bernard Shaw ignored in these plays, to a large extent, the unique opportunities of the dramatist, he also recognised them for what they are. He has always been more interested in his ideas than in his genius. We have no reason to regret it, for we owe him too much; but posterity may think it was unfortunate.

The stage is most fitted to exhibit action, but action without thought and feeling is comparatively uninteresting. The problem of the dramatist is, then, to choose a theme in which thought and feeling can be adequately expressed in action; that is what we mean by a dramatic theme. A conversation can, of course, be dramatic, but it is so in virtue of being part of a story. The most dramatic part of 'St. Joan' was the scene in which Warwick and Cauchon expounded their ideas in our hearing, but what made it so was not merely the interest of listening to those two men speaking out of themselves, but our knowing what hung upon their discussion, the bearing of their talk upon the fate of St. Joan herself.

The same principle holds good of thoughts and feelings, of what we call psychological themes. The inner drama of thoughts and feelings can be as tremendous as any we can see translated in action before our eyes—consider the novels of Dostoievsky, or some of the short stories of Chekov. But only some inner dramas gain more than they inevitably lose by being translated into dialogue and visible movement. Let me take an example.

It was, I think, in the year 1919 that I went to a performance of that excellent, but now defunct, society, the Pioneer Players. They were performing several short plays, and among them a stage version by Mr. Miles Malleson of Chekov's excellent story *The Artist*. It is a short story about a painter and two girls. The girls live with their mother in a country house, near which the artist is dawdling and painting. The play raised the question of the relation of psychology to the stage. It was Mr. Malleson's object to tell in dialogue Chekov's story of the love between the artist and the younger of these two girls. Their love-affair was stopped by the elder of the sisters, who is devoted to good works and regards the artist as a waster, which is partly true. He has no faith in himself. That his work is not more futile than other people's is about the limit of his faith in it; while he is convinced, seeing civilisation is too rotten to be improved by piecemeal remedies, that public-spirited people are fools. Not unnaturally, he and the elder girl hate each other. She discovers her sister's infatuation for this ineligible loafer-artist, and, being ruler in the house, packs off her mother and sister that very night. When the artist returns, only the philanthropic sister is in the house. He hears her voice dictating to a small peasant child. She is teaching it to spell. He hears in the empty house her firm, monotonous voice repeating the sentence again and again, 'And God gave the crow a piece of cheese'. He never sees his love again. In the story the futility of his short romance, and the dreariness of the point of view which has destroyed it, find an echo in that meaningless, reiterated sentence. It is his state of mind, of course, that is the climax of the story; the sense of his own helplessness, the pain of having been pulled out of his faint-hearted loneliness only to to be plunged into it again. Now the printed page can render that state of mind directly, and by describing surroundings reinforce it. But on the stage Mr. Malleson was compelled to make the love-scene all important (for drama is dialogue), and to substitute for Chekov's real climax a dumb scene in which Nicov was shown for a minute reading a letter which tells him his love has gone. That is to say, he was compelled to suggest instead of showing the heart of the theme. All he could get out of such a story on the stage was a clash of two points of view (the artist's and the philanthropist's) and a love-scene of no particular originality. What was most subtle and moving in Chekov's story, therefore, inevitably evaporated on the stage. The drama is a medium of incomparable vividness, but of narrow scope compared with the novel.

Many changes within human beings, such as offer the most interesting themes, are inevitably hidden and silent, or too gradual for drama. 'To penetrate deeply into the human consciousness is the glory of the philosopher, the moralist, the novelist, and, to a certain degree, even of the lyric poet', but the capacity to do so is not enough to make a dramatist. Whatever the temptation, he must not cease to show us something *happening* before our eyes. The stage demands action. When the curtain rises we cease to be possessed alone by a high curiosity. We become also spectators eager to see something happen. 'There are no words so profound or beautiful but they will soon weary us in the theatre if they leave a situation unchanged, if they produce no conflict, no definite solution'.

PROBLEMS OF DIALOGUE

1930

NOW, I ASK YOU TO IMAGINE that you have heard a lecture explaining how the art of modern drama differs from the art of older drama, and what additional burdens and difficulties it compels the artist to shoulder and overcome. In the first place scenic representation has implanted in us a demand that the people should seem as real as the setting. In the second, modern self-consciousness has screwed up the standard of consistency in character-drawing. It has intensified the penetration directed upon character. But, above all, external life has in modern days become less violent, exciting and picturesque. The drama which stands, therefore, for reality in our times as the Greek drama stood for Greek life, and the drama of the Renaissance for the life of the Renaissance, is of necessity less demonstrative. It is possible that some of you have read Maeterlinck's *Le Double Jardin*. I think one may sum up not unfairly one essay in it by saying that whereas the ancients saw tragedy in the sacrifice of Iphigenia or the murder of Agamemnon, and the Elizabethans saw it in the body of Lear lying across the strangled corpse of Cordelia, to the modern audience the spectacle of a family sitting down to tea was full of more terrific elements. That is a travesty of Maeterlinck's conclusions. But it is only a travesty of a truth which he conveys in that essay, namely, that the centre of dramatic interest has shifted for us from demonstrative action to what is happening in people's souls. It follows, therefore, that the dramatist who would do for our times what the older dramatists did for theirs must be an explorer of the inner life.

I propose now to illustrate various ways in which modern dramatists have attempted, through dialogue, to convey a sense of something happening inside the characters on the stage.

Before I go on to illustrate this, consider for a moment the difficulty of the modern dramatist's task. Changes within human beings tend to be hidden and silent. The dramatist has, therefore, to find a sequence of events which will not only account for these changes within, but make those inner changes influence the story that he is telling. And in addition he has to find lines for his characters to speak which will express what is usually hidden and mute—perhaps even unspoken to themselves; while at the same time these lines must be such as the audience recognises as natural and convincing.

Now the modern dramatist who has most noticeably taken advantage of the inexpressiveness of the modern man and woman is Mr. Galsworthy. His chief characteristics as a dramatist are his determination to avoid the theatrical, his sympathy with the social pariah, the unhappily married woman and the victims of justice. Pity is a good thing—possibly there is too much pity in his composition. I cannot go into his treatment of such subjects. The bare mention of them will, I expect, recall his plays. It is as a man of the theatre, not as a thinker—or shall we say sympathiser—that I want to discuss him.

I doubt if he has written a better play than his first, *The Silver Box*. To me, personally, his plays have always been something of a disappointment, though I have not been always insensible to them. The art of presenting character and relations between people on the stage is to suggest that there is much more in people, and between them, than the story actually told can possibly bring out. In this art Mr. Galsworthy seems to me deficient. With a few exceptions his characters, though immediately recognisable as types, lack that background of potentialities we call personality, Mr. Galsworthy draws character as though he had been more interested in 'cases' than individuals. I imagine him as often even withholding his hand from adding a touch which would make a portrait less of a composite photograph, under the influence of a mistaken conscientiousness, which persuades him that loyalty to his theme requires him to work it out in common terms. But in art no one should be commonplace.

Commonplaceness is a category of the generalising, not the artistic mind, and consequently in make-believe such figures have no intense reality. They do not engage our deepest attention, in spite of exhibiting recognisable characteristics. Galsworthy never puts more into his figures than is required for the idea of his play or his satire. He is very sorry for the unfortunate, very just even to those who are in the wrong. He is the ideal magistrate expressing himself in drama. He seems most interested in the representative value of his figures. That a play should have a 'moral,' that the events which we see happening on the stage should have a general bearing on what we have observed in life, that the dramatist's mind should be filled with a sense of the joy and the misery of the world, is all to the good; but only on condition that, when he writes, his interest in these particular people he has created exceeds his interest in anything else. The grumbling over the didactic play is merely a confused way of demanding that the dramatist should be more interested in his characters and their story than what it may suggest to him in the way of general ideas. I know people talk as though no moral could ever be drawn from a genuine work of art, but that is as nonsensical as to suppose that the facts of life cannot suggest one. The more plays we have written by people who are interested in the way the world works, the better, but only pro-

B

vided they are even still more interested in life itself—when it comes to writing about it. Mr. Galsworthy's plays have often reminded me of playing chess against myself. One does not know whether black or white is going to win, for one is playing one's best for both sides, but somehow there is no excitement in the contest. There I have spoken my mind about his drama in general!

What I want to return to is his technique; his determination to avoid at all costs the theatrical, and to tell his story through the medium of the average man or woman's inability to express themselves. You must have been sometimes struck by the literary bleakness of Mr. Galsworthy's dialogue. No one ever expresses himself or herself in his plays better than he or she would have done so in actual life. We are all of us lamentably inexpressive. His plays reflect our inarticulateness. He never improves the occasion. Let me give an example, taken from Mr. Palmer's excellent little book, *The Future of the Theatre*. When the hero of *The Eldest Son*, whose name is Bill, learns from the heroine, whose name is Freda, that she is with child by him, Mr. Galsworthy refuses to improve the occasion. He restricts Freda to saying: 'Oh! Bill!' and makes Bill utter the three following speeches: (1) 'Freda!' (2) 'Good God!' (3) 'By Jove! There is ... ' whereupon the curtain descends and saves him from committing his author any further. These, as Mr. Palmer points out, 'are the tactics of masterly inactivity: The scene is suggested by the players; the audience supplies the emotion; Mr. Galsworthy leaves it at that.'

Now no doubt it is possible to suggest the fantastic genius of man's love for woman and woman's for man by merely making two lovers embrace on the stage, crying out each other's names: 'Harry!' 'Mildred!' But it should be the business of the artist to find words for what Harry and Mildred are feeling, words such as they themselves would recognise, though never find. The dramatist of the first order does so. The dramatist of the highest order of all finds words which, in addition, seem spontaneous and characteristic of them. He makes us believe for the time being that human beings express themselves with a vigour, force and beauty of which, they are, as a matter of fact, quite incapable. In this respect the drama of Shaw is a strong contrast to Galsworthy's and to Granville Barker's. At a Shaw play we recognise what is said as vigorously expressive of each character's point of view. But while they say what they *ought* to have said, if they had had the brains to say it, we are by no means always convinced, as we listen, that those words were natural to them. It is in argument his characters excel; in the expression not of feelings, but of points of view. The heightened dialectical quality of the dialogue is one which distinguishes the plays of Shaw from realistic drama. Mr. Galsworthy has said in a Preface: 'It might be said of Shaw's plays that he creates characters who express feelings which they have not got. It might be said of mine that I create characters who have feelings which they cannot express.' Mr. Galsworthy has also written: 'The English man and woman of to-day have almost a genius for under-expression.' This is his defence of his own method.

Now I should demur at the assertion that in Shaw's plays the characters express feelings they have *not* got; but the dramatist has lent them his own brains to express them. That is to say, in my view, Shaw's dramatic dialogue is superior in kind, though it often falls short of the best dramatic dialogue, because while we listen, however entertained we may be, we often hear the author ventriloquising rather than the characters themselves speaking. Let me take a glaring example. Mr. Doolittle, the dustman in *Pygmalion*, who, you will remember, is Eliza's father and thinks that he may as well take advantage of the fact to touch the professor of Phonetics lightly as a blackmailer line. This is how he is first presented:

DOOLITTLE : Don't say that, Governor. Don't look at it that way. What am I, Governors both? I ask you, what am I? I'm one of the undeserving poor; that's what I am. Think of what that means to a man. It means that he's up agen middle class morality all the time. If there' anything going, and I put in for a bit of it, it's always the same story: 'You're undeserving; so you can't have it.' But my needs is as great as the most deserving

widow's that ever got money out of six different charities in one
week for the death of the same husband. I don't need less than a
deserving man: I need more. I don't eat less hearty than him
and I drink a lot more. I want a bit of amusement, cause I'm a
thinking man. I want cheerfulness and a song and a band when
I feel low. Well, they charge me just the same for everything as
they charge the deserving. What is middle class morality? Just
an excuse for never giving me anything. Therefore, I ask you,
as two gentlemen, not to play that game on me. I'm playing
straight with you. I ain't pretending to be deserving. I'm undeserving; and I mean to go on being undeserving. I like it;
and that's the truth. Will you take advantage of a man's nature
to do him out of the price of his own daughter what he's brought
up and fed and clothed by the sweat of his brow until she's
growed big enough to be interesting to you two gentlemen? Is
five pounds unreasonable? I put it to you; and I leave it to you.

Now it is obvious that in this speech the dramatist has not
tried to imagine how such a character bent on such an errand
would actually express himself, but to put words into his mouth
which will define his attitude towards society, as the dramatist
himself understands it: 'I'm one of the undeserving poor; that's
what I am. Think of what that means to a man. It means that
he's up agen middle-class morality all the time.' That is not a
dustman talking.

In Act V he makes a disgusted appearance in a top-hat and
frock-coat as a lecturer on Moral Reform at £3,000 a year:

DOOLITTLE: It ain't the lecturing I mind. I'll lecture them blue in
the face, I will, and not turn a hair. It's making a gentleman of
me that I object to. Who asked him to make a gentleman of me?
I was happy. I was free. I touched pretty nigh everybody for
money when I wanted it, same as I touched you, Henry Higgins.
Now I am worried; tied neck and heels; and everybody touches
me for money. 'It's a fine thing for you,' says my solicitor. 'Is it?
says I. 'You mean it's a good thing for you,' I says.

Mr Doolittle is a particularly glaring example of a characteristic which runs through Mr. Shaw's dramas. Each speaker is
lent the dramatist's own awareness of the precise orientation of
his ideas or emotions. They are made articulate, but they do not
speak out of themselves so much as explain themselves. The

result is that the audience understands them extremely well but does not believe in them as completely as he comprehends them. The dialogue of Galsworthy and of Shaw are at opposite poles in this respect.

A MASTER OF NATURAL DIALOGUE

1930

CHEKHOV IS AMONG PLAYWRIGHTS the master of dialogue in which characters give themselves away articulately without raising their voices above the pitch of ordinary talk. His people simply speak out of themselves. I propose to remind you first what sort of drama he wrote, that is to say, the kind of states of mind and the kind of emotions he reveals by means of dialogue.

Chekhov follows in the steps of Turgenev: his favourite theme is disillusionment, and above the kind of beauty he creates might well be written 'desolation is a delicate thing.' He is fond of the same kind of settings as Turgenev, too: summer woods, a country house full of cultivated people who talk and talk, in fact *une nichée des gentilhommes*. There you will find the idealist who melts over his own futility, the girl who clutches daily duties tighter in order to forget that youth is sliding away under her feet, the clever man turned maudlin-cynical after his failure to find a purpose in life, the old man who feels he has not yet begun to live, and the old woman who only wants things to go on quietly on humdrum lines. The current of their days is slow; the air they breathe is sultry with undischarged energy, and only broken by unrefreshing nerve storms. It is an atmosphere of sighs, yawns, self-reproaches, vodka, day-dreams, endless tea, endless discussion. These people are like those loosely agglutinated sticks and straws which revolve together slowly in a sluggish eddy. They long to be detached, and ride down the stream which they fancy is somewhere rushing past them. Some day— three hundred, five hundred years hence—perhaps life will be *life*. Ah! those fortunate heirs of the ages who will be alive then! But will they be grateful to their poor predecessors who after all made such glorious life possible? No: they will probably never think of them. That is another reason for self-pity. Stop! This is ridiculous, they argue. What are we doing for them? Nothing. What, indeed, can we do? Nothing, nothing, nothing. Such is the atmosphere in which Chekhov's characters live and move and have their being. It differs from that of Turgenev's generation in being a stuffier air, even less bracing to effort and to hope. There are no Bazarovs to break its spell and bring down the rains of violent tragedy. Tragedy is there, but it is tragedy in the form of a creeping mist which narrows the world to the garden gate. Sometimes the warm wet mist thins away, but it soon closes again, hiding the golden vista of hope for the race.

This is a generalised picture of Chekhov's world. What, you may ask, has it in common with us that it should move us so deeply? Well, I am not convinced that many of us have not after all more in common with these characters than at first sight seems probable. We have more self-control. It is true we are less hysterical, but do not the lives of many when examined resemble that of flies in a glue-pot? Yet it is not only upon this resemblance that the appeal of this drama rests. To watch a Chekhov play is to recapture one's youth; a most uncomfortable yet enviable time when there was intensity even in lassitude, when self-torture did not seem vain; when hope sometimes irradiated and sometimes took the shine out of the present, and when time seemed endless and impossible to fill. 'These people,' the spectator at a Chekhov play finds himself exclaiming, 'are suffering from an unduly protracted youth!' In *Uncle Vanya*, Vanya's elderly passion for the self-centred Elena reflects something of the humiliation of young longing that expects everything and does not understand itself. To all of them, except the meaner, harder sort, it seems that life would be beautiful if, if, if ... With *The Three Sisters* it is '*if* we could get to Moscow'; with the Baron, in that play, '*if* I could find my work'; with Vanya, '*if* only Elena loved me.' And to feel like that is to be, as far as it goes, young. It is, of course, young to want to prop your ladder against a horn of the moon, but it is also to be not quite an adult not to know that although we have immortal hunger in us, there are—a paradox thanks to which the world goes on—satisfying properties in a little real bread. Chekhov's characters have not learnt that. They have a wail in them responsive not only to their own particular frustrations, but to the inevitable disillusionments of life. This quality in Chekhov's work, though it is, as commentators point out, the product of a phase, of a particular period in Russian history, is also a quality which must keep it alive, though not always, of course, acutely interesting. The degree of contemporary interest depends on the degree of wistfulness there may be in the sensibility of any particular generation. But that general theme cannot grow incomprehensible, though it lies behind a picutre of life which in many respects already 'dates.'

Chekhov is the artist of farewells; farewells to youth, to the past, to hopes, to loves. The climax of '*The Cherry Orchard* is a farewell to an old home and all that such a home can mean to the middle-aged; at the end of *Uncle Vanya* the words 'They've gone' uttered by one character after another as they enter after seeing off the professor and his siren wife, are like the tolling of a bell for the burial of passion and excitement.

How does Chekhov get his effects ? He has, of course, like all notable writers, an unerring gift of selecting significant detail. One of the characters says enviously of the author Trigorin in *The Sea-Gull:* 'With him the broken bottle-neck glitters on the dam and the mill-wheel casts a black shadow—and there you have the moonlight night.' That is a gift which cannot be analysed, cannot be taught. Let us take if for granted and pass on. He excels also in creating what is called atmosphere in dialogue. Atmosphere in description needs no definition, but atmosphere in dialogue means that when a group of people are talking together on the stage we are aware of the kind of chord which their separate moods or ideas are making, as though each speaker were a separate note. The mood of the moment, the composite mood of those particular people talking together, is vividly conveyed to us as well as what each speaker is feeling and thinking.

When only two people are talking on the stage this is comparatively easy to achieve (in a love scene, for example), but when a
number of characters are brought together, each sad or happy
for different reasons, and each with different thoughts, who are
nevertheless all involved in the same situation, it needs most
delicate orchestration to give that moment itself a dramatic
character of its own. Of this art Chekhov is a master. He is a
master of the art of setting the mood of one person against that
of another, so that the contrast makes the mood of each more
poignant and interesting. Unfortunately for my purpose, this
faculty can only be illustrated by quotations of considerable
length, I will therefore go on to another characteristic, in
Chekhov's case, closely connected with it.

I have already spoken of the pathetic childlike faith which his
people have that the road on which they are *not* walking is the
best; that somewhere the river of life is rushing sparkling by,
though each feels himself or herself stagnating in a back-water.
Let me take examples from *The Sea-Gull*, though they might be
found in every play Chekhov has written.

By means of subtle contrasts Chekhov shows in that play that
what each character pines for makes no great difference to the
happiness or unhappiness of another who does possess it. Trigorin's talent and adoration of Masha's love for him do not
make him happy, though poor Konstantin shoots himself
because he has neither her love nor her admiration; to be an
actress and the mistress of a great writer bring only misery to
Nina, though in prospect they seemed the gates of heaven to
her. Though Madame Treplev, the successful actress, is blessed
with a thicker skin, no one could call her a happy woman. Her
jealousy of her son's new ideas, even of the young girl who might
possibly win admiration on the stage by interpreting them, the
frantic egotistic clutch with which she holds Trigorin to herself,
her restlessness, stinginess and wild spoilt temper disprove it.
Nor can you call the disillusioned resignation of Dr. Dorn, the
man who has in the eyes of the dying Sorin, 'lived,' happy
either. He has about him just a sufficient touch of kindly stoicism

to throw into relief the distress of the others, but that is all. Women adore him; they have been mad about him. But all his conquests mean to him is a succession of scenes and constant demands on his sympathy. Yet to old Sorin, who wanted love and wanted to write, but had to live alone and earn a living as a magistrate, it seems that Dr. Dorn must be a satisfied man. 'It's all very well for you to argue, 'You've lived your life' (Dorn is much younger), 'but what about me? . . . You've had enough and you don't care, and so you talk like a philosopher but I want to live.' The pathos of this cry lies in his being so near the end of life himself.

Konstantin, again, would give anything for Trigorin's gift, and Nina imagines that to have Trigorin's fame must be the most ecstatic happiness. She is astounded to find that a famous actress should cry at not being able to use the horses one afternoon, and that 'a famous author (Trigorin) adored by the public, written about in all the papers, his photographs for sale, his works translated into foreign languages,' should prefer to spend his time fishing, and be 'delighted at having caught two gudgeon.' When Trigorin shows her what a writer's life amounts to (one of the most interesting passages in the play) she cannot believe a word of it; to her, such life must seem splendid.

It is true that a work of art to have any value must somewhere carry within it the suggestion of desirable life. Where then is that suggestion here? The answer is in the mind of Chekhov himself, in the infection we catch from the spirit of his plays; in the delicate, truthful, humorous, compassionate mind which observes, understands, and forgives.

These people, as I said, are revealing themselves every moment they open their mouths. They do so as completely as in plays old-fashioned in technique, in which the characters soliloquised. Yet Chekhov is a realist, and realistic not only in detail, which was the first form that realism took both in fiction and on the stage. but in his plots which resembled life. Above all, his dialogue resembles real life in its inconsequence. Let me give one example from the first act of *The Cherry Orchard.*

Madame Ranevsky has just returned after a long absence abroad to her old home, with her servants and Anya, her seventeen-year-old daughter. Her brother Gayef, Dunyasha the devoted maid, Barbara her adopted daughter, have been waiting with the intensest excitement for their return.

> BARBARA: How cold it is. My hands are simply frozen, Your two rooms, the white and the violet room, are just the same as they were, mamma.
>
> MADAME RANEVSKY: My nursery, my dear beautiful nursery! This is where I used to sleep when I was a little girl (*crying*). I am like a little girl still (*kissing Gayef and Barbara and then Gayef again*). Barbara hasn't altered a bit, she is just like a nun, and I knew Dunyasha at once (*she kisses D.*).
>
> GAYEF: Your train was two hours late. There's punctuality for you.
> (*Exeunt all but Anya and Dunyasha.*)
>
> ANYA: I've not slept for four nights on the journey. I'm frozen to death.
>
> DUNYASHA: It was Lent when you went away. There was snow on the ground; it was freezing. But now! O my dear (*Laughing and kissing her*), how I've waited for you, my joy, my light! Oh, I must tell you something at once, I can't wait another minute.
>
> ANYA: (*without interest*) What, again?
>
> DUNYASHA: Ephikhodof, the clerk, proposed to me in Easter Week.
>
> ANYA: The same old story ... All my hairpins have dropped out. (*She is very tired.*)
>
> DUNYASHA: I hardly know what to think of it. He loves me. Oh how he loves me!
>
> ANYA (*looking into her bedroom*): My room, my windows, just as if I had never gone away! I'm home again. When I wake in the morning I shall run into the garden, *etc., etc.*

You cannot fail even from this scrap of dialogue to note two things: how it has caught the rhythm of life and in the few words exchanged between the two girls how every word each speaks, instead of answering the other, expresses what each is full of. This is Chekhov's favourite device for letting us into his character's inner feelings. They reply to each other, but they do not so much answer each other as soliloquise. Now, his habit of egotistic relf-revelation is more characteristic of Russian than English character. Therefore English dramatists like Granville Barker,

who are trying to write a dialogue which, while being as collo-
quial as Chekhov's, will be equally self-revealing, have a harder
task.

THE ART OF TELLING A STORY

1930

MY SUBJECT THIS WEEK is the art of telling a story on the stage.
That art has, of course, much in common with the art of telling
stories in print, only the stage demands far greater compression
and the passage of time can only be suggested by the dropping
of the curtain. Consider for a moment what an enormous
difference this makes. In a novel the author can hurry or linger
as he chooses. He can go back in time if he likes, and tell us
what occurred before the events which he presents as actually
happening before our eyes. He can get into the heads of his
characters and tell us what thoughts were in them and what
feelings were in their hearts. If some change of feeling is necessary to account for a change of behaviour he can send him or her
for a walk to thrash matters out, or even round the world, in
order to make his or her subsequent conduct more comprehensible to us. The problem of time exists also for the novelist,
but in a far less crucial manner than it does to the dramatist.
For the dramatist has to tell his story entirely in the present
tense. We must allow him a certain licence in foreshortening
changes in human beings which in order to be true to life require the passage of time. Let me give an example from a
famous play, Ibsen's *Hedda Gabler*. It shows that even the
most conscientious artist may have to sacrifice the letter of truth
in order to be faithful to its spirits. You may remember in that
play that there are two women, one of whom, Hedda, is the bad
angel of a man of genius, while the other Mrs Elfsted, has been
his good angel, weaning him from dissipation and helping him
to write a great book, the MS of which Hedda destroys. Now, in
the play, after the destruction of the manuscript and after the
suicide of Hedda and Lövborg, Tesmann and Mrs Elfsted sit

down on the stage to reconstruct Lövborg's work from his notes. Now nothing is more likely than that Mrs Elfsted should find consolation in this work and marry the futile and industrious Tesmann over it, but since she was devoted enough to run away from her children and brave a scandal in order to look after Lövborg it is certainly not true to life that she would recover in a few minutes from the news of his death sufficiently to start collating and copying. But Ibsen, just before the final dropping of the curtain, wishes to give us a peep into the future and a single incident is all he has time for. Thus, in order to indicate a development which is psychologically consistent he is obliged to represent one of his characters behaving in a way which is, at the moment, psychologically false. This is a dilemma which lies in wait for the psychological dramatist at every turn. It is one of the principle difficulties of telling an intricate story on the stage.

In the art of telling a story, whether on the stage or in print, the beginning is very important. Only whereas the novelist can often afford to open in a leisurely way, the fact that the dramatist has only about two hours and a half to three hours in which to tell everything forces him to hurry from the start. If you examine poor plays you will notice that the dramatist has often been too long in getting under weigh. The art of stage craft is to a large extent the art of expounding character and situation by employing means which at the same time carry the story along. If you recall the opening scene of *Hamlet*, you will notice it is a dive into the centre of the situation which is to be developed. It opens with the cry of the sentry on the platform of the Castle of Elsinore, and immediately we are aware that Horatio and Marcellus are there to confirm with their own eyes the rumour of the ghost. Their speculations upon the meaning of this apparition and what they ought to do, at once inform the audience of the state of affairs in Denmark. Let me take another, and perhaps still more striking example of an opening as mystifying and as significant of what is to come. When the curtain rises upon the first act of Ibsen's *Rosmersholm* we find ourselves in the hall of an old country house, where everything is dignified and quiet, speaking of the old established order. There are two women in this room, and they are waiting for the return of the master of the house. One is a beautiful young woman with a great deal of life in her, and the other is a staid old house-keeper. The elderly woman, looking out of the window sees that the master is approaching, and exclaims with astonish-ment, 'he is coming over the bridge!'—an exclamation which is greeted by the younger with incredulous and eager joy. She too goes to the window, and then she is disappointed: after all he is going round the other way. Our interest is at once excited. Why should such a little thing as that mean so much to these two women? Gradually we learn what Rosmer's crossing the bridge would have meant to Rebecca. It was that bridge from which Rosmer's wife flung herself into the mill-stream, pushed to-wards suicide by the subtlest hints by Rebecca herself. Rebecca had entered Rosmer's world as a ruthless adventuress; she had seen that his hysterical wife was a millstone round his neck; she was aware, much more aware than Rosmer himself, of her own power over him; she meant to marry him and make herself a leader in politics and society by using him as a means to power. But she did not reckon with the Rosmer conscience. Rosmer when the play begins is unaware of her past machina-tions and of the part which she played in the tragedy which still haunts him. If he had come home that morning by the bridge with its terrible associations it would have been a sign that he had begun to forget the past and that she might still triumph.

That is the way to begin a story on the stage. Only in the course of the action which hurries towards its final catastrophe do we gradually gather the facts about the past which make that catastrophe natural, so that we can understand the refusal of Rebecca to marry Rosmer, but her willingness to fling herself into the mill-stream with him at the end. Ibsen is the master of this kind of gradual revelation. Whatever happens next before our eyes implies something which has happened before the play itself began, which is at every turn imparted just in time to give the next incident its utmost significance. This is the perfection of dramatic story-telling. The secret of a story for the stage is, then, to begin in the middle and gradually allow the audience to become aware that there is in the past of the characters exhibited stuff enough for other unseen dramas.

Let me take another example of a storyteller's skill. Sir James Barrie is exceedingly adept at telling a story on the stage, and did he not possess this faculty his fantasias would not hold together in the way they do. You probably remember *The Admirable Crichton*. It shows that when a dramatist has found a significant, fundamental idea the problem of story-telling is enormously simplified. The theme of *The Admirable Crichton* is as simple as that of any *conte philosophique* by Voltaire. It is, that if we were to return to 'nature' the relative importance of human beings would be startlingly reversed. In Act I we are introduced to an elderly peer who has a theoretic belief in equality and insists on once a month treating his servants as though they were honoured guests. His butler, Mr Crichton, is the only servant who is not sadly embarrassed by this, and he hints that treating servants as equals is not equivalent to 'a return to nature'. In London, he says, it is 'natural' for earls to be earls and for servants to be servants. In Act II we are shown what 'the return to nature' really is, for the earl and his family and servants, yachting on the South Seas, are wrecked on a desert island, whereupon the relative position of everybody is changed. Crichton assumes ascendancy, at first quite unconsciously; he is the only practical man. In Act III two years have passed and he has become the king of the little community, and the earl has cheerfully descended to menial offices. But the appearance of a steamer at the island at once reverses everybody's position again. In the last act they are all once more in London, and Crichton, who on the island was prepared to make the earl's daughter an exceedingly proud and happy woman, settles down with 'the tweenie' in a little pub in Harrow Road. Now here the idea has provided at a blow the outline of the story. All the dramatist has had to do is to employ his invention in manufacturing details which will bring each turn in the situation ironically home. It is a good example of the truth that if the dramatist can think of a good, simple idea, a story on the stage tells itself.

I should like before I stop to take one more example, again from the plays of Sir James Barrie, to show how important the art of story-telling is when the supernatural is concerned or the theme is a delicate one. In *Mary Rose* he had to make us believe for the time being that a young woman might disappear from the world and come back after twenty-five years as young as ever. The curtain went up on a dark dismantled drawing-room of a bereaved uninhabited house. A robust Australian soldier is heard questioning the caretaker. She is a shivery, thin, apprehensive creature, starting at every creak of the dusty boards, and she obviously has much on her mind. The Australian says he is a grandson of the people who once lived there. He gets her to confess reluctantly that the house is haunted and sends her down to the kitchen to make him a cup of tea. While she is away he grows, in spite of himself, uneasy; the door behind him slowly opens and closes; he does not see that, but from his movements we guess that he feels some presence is there in the dusk, or making dim signs to him out of its own darkness or horror. He shakes himself together and sits down by the empty grate to wait for his tea. In the last scene we see him still sitting there. Meanwhile the lives of his grandfather and grandmother, of his mother and his father, before he was born, pass before his mind. It is these events we see (Act I, Scene 2, Act II, and Act III, Scene 1). His mother is Mary Rose, who was spirited away on the Enchanted Island four years after his birth. We see her return after twenty-five years to an altered world, where those she loved are now old. It was more than she could bear, and (presumably) she vanished again. Still she keeps coming back again, searching in misery for her little boy who had run away from home. Mary Rose, of course, is the ghost who haunts the house, and in the last scene she is confronted by her son, who knows who she is but whom she does not recognise, in whom indeed she would be horrified to recognise her little Harry.

Now, in putting the story of the play out of time, by suggesting that all we see and hear is taking place in the mind of that Australian soldier sitting in a battered chair in an empty room, the dramatist makes it easier for us to yield temporary consent to the fantastic machinery of his story. We begin with a shiver of the supernatural; consequently, the weird music at the picnic on the island, audible only to the ears of Mary Rose, afterwards finds with us a more easy reception. And that we know what is ahead of these amiable, simple people lends pathos to their trivialities, their joys and their affection for each other. We watch them with more intensity than we otherwise would, and also with a half-ironic tenderness. Mary Rose exclaims at one point that she wished we knew when things were happening for the last time, for then we should value them much more—a thought everybody has had. Well, we know these things *are* happening to them for the last time, and that this cosy, gay safe life they are living is soon going to pass away. Such is the art of the story-teller.

SYMBOLISM ON THE STAGE

1930

SYMBOLISM HAS NEVER BEEN MUCH employed by English dramatists. The English genius runs to poetry or to matter-of-factness. Dramatic symbolism is usually a compromise between the two. There are two types of symbolistic plays. In the first the whole play is symbolic of human life; in the second, some figure or thing or event has more than its literal value. The earliest English drama, the morality plays, were entirely symbolic; 'Everyman is of these the most famous. But most of the more remarkable modern symbolist dramas have been foreign importations. There is, for example, a Russian play by Evréistof called *The Theatre of the Soul*, once nearly performed at the Alhambra. Its performance was, however, cancelled at the last moment owing to the manager discovering in it a repulsive incident: a woman's wig is taken off and her bald head is displayed.

The woman in question is 'a concept,' not a real person; for all the personages in this play are only symbols of what goes on in the soul; the soul, or Whole Man, being the stage on which they appear and struggle together. She, the woman, is first invoked by the romantic, sensual side of Man and appears before us as a radiant figure; then her image is summoned up by his Reason. The difference between the two visions is symbolised by her taking off her wig and displaying a bald head and pulling out a dental plate. Then a contest (still representative of what goes on in Man, who is himself the stage) takes place between her image and the image of the man's wife. Invoked by Reason, the wife appears as a pathetic and dignified figure; afterwards, invoked by the romantic, sensual side of Man, as a nagging, narrow, joyless, draggle-tailed, grasping shrew. The radiant concept gets the other down; but the romantic side of his nature is disappointed in the end, and we are given to understand that 'the Man' shoots himself. At least, the red, throbbing light which at the back of the scene has·represented all along his physical heart, suddenly goes out, and the figure, who has stood for the romantic, sensual side of his nature, is seen drowning in streamers of red ribbon.

The drama thus consists of a dialogue between the two figures who represent Reason and Romantic Sensuality respectively. Matters are complicated by the fact that they share the same nervous system, and each suffers when the other gets control of the machine. The chief difficulty, so it strikes me, in staging this symbolic play would be to find an adequate symbol for the nervous system. Reason in Man is constantly crying out to the romantic sensualist, 'Keep your hands off my nerves!' 'Don't touch then!' There is also a third personage present on the stage, who is dressed in worn traveller's clothes and represented as sound asleep during all these wrangles. This is 'The Unconscious Self.' (It pleases me to see this hypothesis, about which there is so much dubious chatter going on, relegated to its proper place.) When 'The Man' dies by the hand of the romantic sensualist in him, a railway porter comes in with a lantern

C

and says, 'This is Everyone's Town. You have to get out here, sir. You change here.' 'Thank you, yes,' says the Unconscious Self. 'I have to change here,' and he follows the porter, yawning.

Well, this is an example of a play in which every figure, every event and even the scenery is symbolic. Allegory rather than symbolism is really a better word for describing such plays. Their merit depends either on the poetry they contain or upon the intellectual ingenuity with which they interpret experience. In this case there is little or no poetry.

The Insect Play, by the brothers Capek, is a far more satisfying piece of work from both points of view. It is a satire on humanity. There is only one human being in it, a tramp; all the other characters are insects, who represent human types.

In the first act of *The Insect Play* we watch the flitter-flutter courtship of human butterflies. The object of the authors is not to emphasise the charm, but the uninteresting instinctiveness of their pursuit of each other and their matings. Thus, instead of sipping the essence of flowers, the human butterflies stimulate their quivering, impatient excitement at a refreshment bar, and then—it does not matter really which one couples with which— each pair sinks into the euthanasia of a matter-of-fact love-death. . . .

The Tramp, who plays the part of Chorus, represents poor, ragged, Rational Humanity throughout the play. He is disgusted at this purposeless spectacle of butterfly-love. But, when the curtain rises on this next vision, the parallel in the insect world to 'serious' as opposed to amorous careers, his disgust, if anything intensifies. He sees, and we see, the dung beetles (admirable grotesques!) rolling and patting their ball of dirt; no light sinners these, but steady folk.

Mr. BEETLE: Our capital—that's what it is—our lovely capital— careful—careful.

Mrs. BEETLE: Can't be too careful with our capital—our little pile.

But while Mr. Beetle is away looking for a safe hole in which to hide the precious ball, a robber beetle comes and trundles it off. We see also a more adventurous type in whom the acquisitive instinct is uppermost in another form, Mr. Ichneumon Fly, who is a born assassin with a dagger. Plunder, not hoarding, is his instinctive passion. But he is a worker in his way, too. He expounds his views to the Tramp. 'Up early, home late, but, as long as you're doing it for someone worth doing it for, what does it matter? Am I right?' (He is a devoted father, nourishing on the tit-bits of corpses an extremely unpleasant little larva of a daughter.) 'And how it cheers us up when you do your duty like that. Do the job that's nearest though it's dull at whiles. When you feel that, you feel you are not living in vain. . . . Brains, expert knowledge, enterprise, imagination, initiative . . .' We see his victims too, little Mr. and Mrs. Cricket, who only want to chirp away their lives in roseate, harmless domesticity. But the brothers Capek hold the balance true. They do not spare the triviality of the Cricket's mutual endearments, the feeble tinkle of their egotistic merriment over the fate of another Cricket whose house they inherit, and who was snapped up by a bird. Yet, like the Tramp, we feel a pang of pity when the helpless little creatures are stilettoed by the bounding, active Ichneumon, and we are hardly sorry when Parasite, a ragged, idle rascal, whose motto is 'Down with larders, storing is robbing,' emerges from that ill-omened home, bulging with the swallowed larva. 'Gah! Bleedin' Bolshie,' is the Tramp's comment on the Parasite.

> These 'ere Insec's never dream
> Of workin' to some general scheme.

Next time he dreams his head is on an ant-heap. Now we see a 'selfless' community, but that spectacle also is not cheering. It is a satire upon heroic State-and-Army civilisation. During this scene there is one character which takes no part in the action. It is a Chrysalis, who stands, like a little grey mummy, at the side of the stage, uttering from time to time in a sweet, youthful voice sentiments of purest hope and confidence. When she is born, she says, the whole world will be changed.

'One, two, three, four.' A blind ant in goggles squats, beating the time to which slaves of the State move like machines. Wires rule the sky, chimneys and poles rise against it; the ground is trampled brown. 'One, two, three, four.' All for the Whole! The master of Time will master the world! Speed the output! Quicker, quicker! '*Blank*, three four.' Through the mouths of two engineers the philosophy of the Human Ant Heap is bawled at us in the staccato of heroes. Peace means work! He who works possesses more, requires more, has more to defend. Work! Strength! War! Great is Science and it will prevail; nothing serves the State like Science! We must have that bit of the world now from the Birch to the Pine Tree; we, or the Yellows. They have insulted us! War! War is forced upon us! To arms! the din increases; the Engineer-Dictator-Emperor shouts commands; the telegraph clicks out news of victories, and of retreats 'according to plan.' Groaning wounded are borne across the stage; and female ants, selling flags, collect pennies for them. The Journalist keeps up the Heap's morale. A fourth army is destroyed, but a fifth takes its place. Splendid! Victory at last is ours! The Dictator kneels in gratitude to the Great God of Ants and appoints him an honorary colonel. More din, more confusion. Now *our* armies are flying! Send the unfit to the front! Mobilise the nation! Alas, all is in vain. The Yellows have taken the city! 'Fight, fight on!,' roars the leaders. 'After them—murder them all!' roars back the Yellow captain; and he, in turn, kneels to the most righteous God of Ants—'Thou knowest that we fight only for justice, honour and our commercial interests.' But this is more than the Tramp can stand. 'Bah! Yer insect,' he shouts, as he stamps him flat.

The Tramp wakes, sick and shivering, in the dark. The wood is full of voices: 'I am wounded'—'Water'—'Aha! Got 'em (that must be the voice of the Ichneumon still at work.) 'Iris, Iris, I love you.'—'My pile, my pile.'—'Army of occupation, advance.' Day begins to peep and Mayflies to dance in the early sun rays. The Chrysalis bursts forth from her cerements, and with a cry of esctasy joins them. One by one the happy little creatures hail life, and die. Is *this* the secret of life?—the Tramp asks himself.

They seem to die as rapturously as they lived. And our particular Mayfly? Her turn soon comes. She stops dancing, intending to tell us the secret of life—and softly she, too, lies down and dies.

Now to turn to the other type of dramatic symbolism, to those realistic plays in which some incident or object or character is stressed in a peculiar way, with the intention of suggesting something more than itself. This method, which can be extremely effective, is exceedingly difficult to manage, and unless it is beautifully done, the results are disastrous. Ibsen, after all, is far and away the greatest of all modern dramatists, and it is Ibsen who affords the most illuminating examples of this kind of symbolism. There are moments in his dramas when the human figures, whose motives have been revealed with psychological matter-of-factness, become luminous and transparent, so that we are aware of the forces they represent, and the words they speak become expressive of their ambiguous condition. Sometimes, on the other hand, he frankly introduced a symbolic non-human figure to achieve this effect; the Rat Wife in *Little Eylof*, for example, who enters a solid suburban home. When these moments occur (they are frequent in the later dramas) it is important that the producer should explain to the actors that, however solidly real they have been till then, they are *now* also voices speaking from the depths of human nature. To modulate out of psychological, prosaic drama into poetic, symbolic drama puts an enormous strain both upon the actors and the production; yet at those moments the beauty of Ibsen's work is at stake. Such a moment is the dual suicide in the play I mentioned last week, *Rosmersholm*.' And there is another moment just before, in which a minor figure—Brandel, a sort of little Peer Gynt, should appear with the effect of a phantom. He crosses the stage twice. The first time merely as a megalomaniac dreamer, who is at last going to thunder out his message to the world, to scatter his hoarded gold of thought. Utter sham though he is (he helped to educate Rosmer years before), he gives a fillip to the courage of his old pupil, enabling Rosmer to stand up for a while to domineering conventionalism. (Sham prophets like Brandel often stimulate for a little while people sincerer than themselves.) The second time he appears as a self-confessed failure. He has become a shabby spectre of all bankrupt aspirations—and as such he then helps to undermine Rosmer's tottering faith in his own aspirations. Brandel should be on his second appearance almost as uncanny a figure as the Rat Wife, who, besides being an old ratcatcher with a terrier in a bag, is also 'death.'

In the old days there was much discussion about the legitimacy of Ibsen's use of symbols. I think we are all of one mind now: *everything is legitimate in art that really comes off*. The only question is what kind of a symbol is most likely to make its effect. In my opinion, the introduction of the Rat-wife makes too sudden and violent demand upon our suspension of disbelief. Ibsen shows himself a greater master of his craft when he uses a real human being. Brandel, with the effect of a spectre of lost illusions. Or in *The Wild Duck* (to my mind the most perfect of all his plays), where the wounded bird in its garret, among withered Christmas trees and tame rabbits, suggests first the broken life of old Ekdal—that tendency in all wounded men and women to cower down into a nest of dreams away from realities, and lastly the small girl herself who is brought up in this contented, but stuffy, home. The symbolism here has several facets; so, too, has the Rat Wife, who, if she is death, also symbolises those shameful desires to be rid of those who, if loved, are also burdens. The Rat Wife symbolises all secret wishes to which people dare not own.

But note this difference. Whereas in *Little Eylof* we, the audience, have to interpret the symbol and make it do its work, in the case of *The Wild Duck* that is done for us by the characters in the play. It is in the speeches of Gregers Werle, whose enigmatic, dark sayings are a proper part of his spiritual pretensions, and in the queer fancies of a dreamy child, that the significance of its symbolism is disclosed. That is more masterly stagecraft.

Can we draw any conclusions as to the proper use of symbols in drama? Allegory stands, of course, on its own feet. Where everything is a symbol the interest, coherence and the pointfulness of the criticism of life implied are the only tests. But the symbolic treatment of details in a realistic picture of life is another matter. It is the shortest and yet the most risky method of modulating out of realism into poetry, of suggesting that life, though it seems ordinary, is mysterious. It cannot therefore be handled by anyone in whom the sense of mystery is not genuine and, I think, we may add, original—for nothing is more flat than a well-worn symbol. Lastly, the example of Ibsen shows that when its significance is the result of the play of imagination in the characters themselves, and the symbol is not something addressed to the audience alone, it is doubly effective.

DICTION AND REALISM

1930

I TOUCHED ON THE QUESTION OF DICTION, if you remember, in discussing the dialogue of Galsworthy and Shaw; in that context mixed with character creation, I said that Mr. Galsworthy's characters tended often to be personifications of averages, and Mr. Shaw's of opinions. The diction of a personified average is inevitably dim and threadbare; the diction of a personified opinion, on the other hand, may have a spirited rhetorical ring about it. Such speeches may abound in smashing retorts and sudden surprises. And this is certainly true of Mr. Shaw's dramatic diction. He has written the most exhilarating harangues of our time. But although unmatched for energy and point, I think you will find no passages in his plays in which when you listen to them you cannot tell whether it is the thought or the word which has moved you, or whether they can be separated at all—and that is the test. He has attempted now and then an eloquence intended to move us by a fine excess. Here is the speech of Mrs. George, for example, in *Getting Married*. I think you will agree it does not achieve its proper excellence so surely as many of his argumentative harangues.

Mrs. GEORGE (*with intensely sad reproach*): When you loved me, I gave you the whole sun and stars to play with. I gave you eternity in a single moment, strength of the mountains in one clasp of your arms, and the volume of all the seas in one impulse of your soul. A moment only; but was it not enough? Were you not paid then for all the rest of your struggle on earth? Must I mend your clothes and sweep your floors as well? Was it not enough? I paid the price without bargaining: I bore the children without flinching: was that a reason for heaping fresh burdens on me? I carried the child in my arms: must I carry the father, too? When I opened the gates of paradise, were you blind? was it nothing to you? When all the stars sang in your ears and all the winds swept you into the heart of heaven, were you deaf? were you dull? was I no more to you than a bone to a dog? Was it not enough? We spent eternity together; and you ask me for a little lifetime more. We possessed all the universe together; and you ask me to give you my scanty wages as well. I have given you the greatest of all things; and you ask me for my body as a plaything. Was it not enough? Was it not enough?

I should be sorry if you did not admire that passage. I should be sorry, also, if you did not feel that it falls short of the finest imaginative prose. It is, of course, purely rhetorical in movement and the sun, the stars, the mountains, when they are mentioned to lend grandeur to the pleading, are the tokens of an orator not the images of a poet. They were not, one feels, present to the senses of the writer. Still, Shaw moving with such energy and freedom in the world of ideas, has been less hampered than other dramatists by the dingy threadbare language in which the characters in modern realistic drama are forced to express themselves. It is, of course, the poets who have regretted most this compulsion. Those who are dramatists among them know that drama must be founded on living speech, and that to avoid common language by writing with elaboration what could not have been spoken, is death to drama. They want a living idiom in which they could write imaginatively without too much picking and choosing of words, confident that in that idiom emotion

might be trusted to bring forth the right one. This was the
great hope of the Irish Dramatic Movement. They had discovered such an idiom in the English-speaking but Irish-think-
ing peasant. The plays of Synge show it. In this short preface
to *The Play Boy of the Western World*, after telling us that he
has used only one or two words he had not heard among the
country people of Ireland, and that anyone who has lived in real
intimacy with the Irish peasantry knows that the wildest sayings
and ideas in his plays are tame compared with the fancies one
may hear in any little hillside cabin, he goes on to say:

All art is a collaboration; and there is little doubt that in the
happy ages of literature, striking and beautiful phrases were as
ready to the story-teller's or the playwright's hand, as the rich
cloaks and dresses of his time. It is probably that when the Elizabethan dramatist took his ink-horn and sat down to his work he
used many phrases that he had just heard, as he sat at dinner, from
his mother or his children. In Ireland, those of us who know the
people have the same privilege. When I was writing *The Shadow
in the Glen* some years ago, I got more aid than any learning could
have given me from a chink in the floor of the old Wicklow house
where I was staying, that let me hear what was being said by the
servant girls in the kitchen. This matter, I think, is of great importance, for in countries where the imagination of the people, and the
language they use, is rich and living, it is possible for a writer to
be rich and copious in his words, and at the same time to give the
reality, which is the root of all poetry, in a comprehensive and
natural form. In the modern literature of towns, however, richness
is only found in sonnets, or prose poems, or in one or two elaborate
books that are far away from the profound and common interests
of life. One has, on one side, Mallarmé and Huysmans producing
this literature; and on the other Ibsen and Zola dealing with the
reality of life in joyless and pallid words. On the stage one must
have reality, and one must have joy; and that is why the intellectual modern drama has failed, and people have grown sick of the
false joy of musical comedy, that has been given them in place of
the rich joy found only in what is superb and wild in reality. In a
good play every speech should be as fully flavoured as a nut or an
apple, and such speeches cannot be written by anyone who works
among people who have shut their lips on poetry. In Ireland, for a
few years more, we have a popular imagination that is fiery, and

magnificent and tender; so that those of us who wish to write start with a chance that is not given to writers in places where the spring-time of the local life has been forgotten, and the harvest is a memory only, and the straw has been turned into bricks.

Let me remind you of this speech which is as fully flavoured as a nut or an apple. The passage I am about to quote occurs in the second act of *The Play Boy of the Western World*. The girls have heard that Christy Mahon is at the inn. They have heard rumours that he is a wonder and a savage man. Christy is easy to flatter. He has not been able to resist telling them of his mighty blow which clove his father's skull. Pegeen is jealous and tries to frighten him.

CHRISTY (*very miserably*): Oh, God help me. Are you thinking I'm safe? You were saying at the fall of night I was shut of jeopardy and I here with yourselves.

PEGEEN (*severely*): You'll be shut of jeopardy no place if you go talking with a pack of wild girls the like of them do be walking abroad with the peelers, talking whispers at the fall of night.

CHRISTY (*with terror*): And you're thinking they'd tell?

PEGEEN (*with mock sympathy*): Who knows, God help you?

CHRISTY (*loudly*): What joy would they have to bring hanging to the likes of me?

PEGEEN: It's queer joys they have, and who knows the thing they'd do, if it'd make the green stones cry itself to think of you sway-ing and siggling at the butt of a rope, and you with a fine, stout neck, God bless you! the way you'd be a half an hour, in great anguish, getting your death.

CHRISTY (*getting his boots and putting them on*): If there's that terror of them, it's be best, maybe, if I went on wandering like Esau or Cain and Abel on the sides of Neifen or the Erris plain.

PEGEEN (*beginning to play with him*): It would, maybe, for I've heard the Circuit Judges this place is a heartless crew.

CHRISTY (*bitterly*): It's more than Judges this place is a heartless crew. (*Looking up at her*) And isn't it a poor thing to be starting again, and I a lonesome fellow will be looking out on women and girls the way the needy fallen spirits do be looking on the Lord?

PEGEEN: What call have you to be that lonesome when there's poor girls walking Mayo in their thousands now?

CHRISTY (*grimly*): It's well you know what call I have. It's well you know it's a lonesome thing to be passing small towns with the lights shining sideways when the night is down, or going in strange places with a dog noising before you and a dog noising behind, or drawn to the cities where you'd hear a voice kissing and talking deep love in every shadow of the ditch, and you passing on with an empty, hungry stomach failing from your heart.

PEGEEN: I'm thinking you're an odd man, Christy Mahon. The oddest walking fellow I ever set my eyes on to this hour to-day.

CHRISTY: What would any be but odd men and they living lonesome in the world?

PEGEEN: I'm not odd, and I'm my whole life with my father only.

CHRISTY (*with infinite admiration*): How would a lively, handsome woman the like of you be lonesome when all men should be thronging around to hear the sweetness of your voice, and the little infant children should be pestering your steps, I'm thinking, and you walking the roads.

PEGEEN: I'm hard set to know what way a coaxing fellow the like of yourself should be lonesome either.

CHRISTY: Coaxing.

PEGEEN: Would you have me think a man never talked with the girls would have the words you've spoken to-day? It's only letting on you are to be lonesome, the way you'd get around me now.

CHRISTY: I wish to God I was letting on; but I was lonesome all times, and born lonesome, I'm thinking, as the moon of dawn.

Such is the quality of this diction. Person after person in these laughing, sorrowful, ironic plays is 'the like of the little children do be listening to the stories of an old woman, and do be dreaming after in the dark night its' in grand houses of gold they are, with speckled horses to ride, and do be waking again in a short while and they destroyed with the cold, and the thatch dripping, may be, and the starved ass braying in the yard.' The heart of these plays is the contrast of the dream within and the meagre reality without; and it is alternately out of the shining dream and a rasping shrewdness that the characters in them speak. But the point for me at this moment is not the queer duality of Irish character, but the fact that it is expressed in language uncorrupted either by schoolmasters or newspapers; and that what is present to the minds is also present to the senses when they speak. The result is a joyful, fantastic, extravagant, beautiful and altogether reckless manner of speech.

Here is a language which rises out of common life. But is it only in works of bookish poets or the peasant that we can find in it? Mr. Max Beerbohm when he was a dramatic critic once wrote that a play cannot have style because the people must talk in it as they talk in daily life. He was thinking of the play made out of educated or semi-educated modern life where speech is no longer vivid. It has not been done in our time. Perhaps Oscar Wilde came near finding such a substitute for the pallid chatter of the drawing-room, just missing it because he would sharpen every line into a point. When we attend a play by Congreve and in a lesser degree by Sheridan, it is undoubtedly the finished ease of every phrase which adds exhilaration to the entertainment. Have you not felt the relief, the release of listening to dialogue which apart from the sparkle of wit upon it is both voluble and precise? The only picturesque talk to-day, so rapidly is that doubtful boon education ironing out our minds, is slang. And slang is stereotyped language—except in the mouths of some Americans, concealing more character than it reveals. Yet the realistic play, if it is to live, must have style. I have, in conclusion, only one other word to say about realism. Realism is only a means not an end. It is only a method of making us believe in what is happening before our eyes on the stage, whether it be realism of scenery, speech or gesture. The mimicry of life is of no value in itself, and belief can be created by other means as well. Nor is this strange when we remember that the whole of art is an appeal to a reality which is not without us but in our minds.

SHAKESPEARE

A MID-SUMMER NIGHT'S
DREAM
THE PRODUCTION OF POETIC DRAMA

1914

B EFORE CRITICIZING THE performance at the Savoy Theatre
I must (I apologize) discourse on the production of poetic
drama in general.

A Midsummer Night's Dream is a difficult play to produce so
that everybody shall find in it satisfaction, and it is hard to find
out what one wants. In the theatre that each playgoer carries
under his own hat, it has already been performed, perhaps
several times and in several ways. We are our own scene makers
and shifters in that theatre, and what easy miracles we perform!
The action takes place amidst surroundings more vague and
changeable than clouds; the scenery paints itself, as we read,
upon the darkness of the mind, a more suggestive background
for beauty than any decorative curtain. Indeed, can we even say
that anything definite is painted on that darkness at all? We *feel*
as we read; we have hardly time to see. Did we see anything
when we read, for instance:

> Met we on hill, or dale, forest or mead,
> By paved fountain or by rushy brook,
> Or in the beached margent of the sea,
> To dance our ringlets to the whistling wind?

We were charmed, but did we *see* what charmed us? Now you
put the question to yourself you may, at the words 'rushy
brook', see rushes and water for a hundredth of a second; and
'the beached margent of the sea' may call up for an instant a
scene before you. Indeed, as I wrote down the above lines they
called up one for me: the moon is up, but it is not night; a sea,
green as the stalks of daffodils, spills softly wave after wave

over smooth white sand. But how utterly irrelevant such details are! Next time I may see a different shore or nothing at all. I can even trace to their sources these particular irrelevancies. I happen to have spent a month this summer on the coast of Wexford; 'rushy' in the previous line must have lingered in my mind and made me think of the reedy grasses which grow on the dunes there, and then of the magic emptiness of that beach one evening, and the little, tossing fringes of fresh foam running in, more fraily white than snow, one after the other. How recklessly the imagination picks and jumps and chooses! There was not a suggestion of 'the whistling wind' in my picture, on the contrary, a warm stillness; though the dancing and the fairies and their ringlets were somehow there—in the foam.

Again, what different dawns the following lines will call up to different minds, at different times:

> Even till the Eastern gate, all fiery red,
> Opening in Neptune with fair blessed beams
> Turns into yellow gold his salt green streams.

In my picture there may be a headland—I may be seeing England on a summer morning from the sea; you may be looking upon a broad, restless circle of empty water, a path of gold across it to the rising sun; another reader, a green swell heaving against the sky, catching on its side a golden light. And another may see nothing at all.

The poet has written what he has written, and we have all found different things upon the page. But our various experiences have this in common: a *feeling* of morning and the sea. It does not matter that this feeling should be centred in one case upon one deatil, in another upon another. The important fact is that each vision has a certain consonance with sea and morning and that the poetry has created in us a capacity to feel (this is the only test of poetry) the beauty of whatever picture or idea the words happened to call up.

Such psychological facts are not unrelated to the art of the theatre. They suggest the limits of the art of interpreting poetry with dress and scenery on the stage, and a standard by which to criticize it. They suggest that this art, like the art of words, should leave us to a great extent fancy free. What scenery should aim at is the expression of a beauty consonant with the underlying emotion which runs through the poetry of a scene, act, or play.

There are, of course, some people whose imaginations demand absolute freedom. To them any attempt to express emotion visibly is irksome; and they, too, go to Shakespeare performances sometimes, sitting through them with resigned patience. Perhaps, for their benefit, goggles might be procurable for a shilling in the slot, as opera-glasses are now for others. Certainly the producer can do nothing more for them than that; he cannot be expected to consider people who want *only* to use their ears in the theatre.

But, clearly if we are to be left to a great extent fancy free, the staging of poetic drama should not tie or direct our imaginations too definitely. That it should be beautiful in itself no producer denies; but if it is added that it must also possess a beauty consonant with the spirit of the act or scene they are all at sixes and sevens—at any rate in their practice. And well they may be. For what is meant by the beauty of stuffs, colours, forms and light being consonant with the beauty of the poetry is something extremely vague. Suggestion of place, of night or day, is another matter and a simpler one. The scene must always be laid somewhere, and this must be indicated, if only by a symbol or an announcement. The attitude towards scenery of different schools of producers are discussed and distinguished in Mr. Palmer's *Future of the Theatre*. Beauty in the setting of a play must, he asserts, detract from dramatic art, which is 'the realisation through the living player of the conceptions of a dramatic poet'. 'It is psychologically impossible', he says, 'to receive more than one appeal at a time.' I deny this generalisation, and with an energy which, if he could see my gesture, he might mistake for personal animosity. He appeals to our experience, and instances Purcell's setting of one of Shakespeare's songs. *Santo Diavolo!* I am unconvinced! I will appeal to his

D

experience. Has he never been glad a beautiful song has been sung in an unintelligible language, not because the poetry was too good but because it was too bad? Has he never glanced at a programme translation afterwards with a sense of relief at what he had providentially missed?

I know a man who heard a lady sing a pretty song he thought was about an Indian potentate called Sir Cusha Sweesong Twar. Unfortunately, when he discovered that the refrain was '*Ce que je suis sans toi*', I neglected to ask him if the song appealed to him more, but probably, in this instance, on either alternative his answer would have been another nail in the coffin of Mr Palmer's theory that good words and good music inevitably spoil each other. And as for his twin theory that what delights the eye and charms the fancy in stage settings must subduct from the poetry of drama, and his deduction from it that the scenery for Shakespeare must be so conventional, so much in every detail a matter of course as to become psychologically invisible like Mr Chesterton's postman in his detective story, they leave us in a pretty quandary. For it follows that it is impossible to produce Shakespeare at all. As he points out, Mr Poel's more or less archaeological method of staging the plays, though it may get near the bare stage conventions of Shakespeare's time, is so strange to ours that it needs a 'complicated mental gymnastic' on our part 'before we can begin to see and appreciate the play'. We must, however—this is granted—indicate time and place on the stage. But then what hopeless difficulty we are in! If we have no scenery, then we cannot attend to the play; if we have elaborate naturalistic scenery we are distracted; and if the producer 'decorates', instead of 'illustrates', he is calling in a conflicting element of beauty.

How can we establish a convention as stable, and therefore as unnoticeable, as the Greek stage was to the Greeks? If we build a Shakespeare theatre for that purpose, would not its bare, unchanging platform prove also distracting to an audience which frequented other theatres in which every degree of realism and abstract decoration was in vogue? I know I am pressing Mr

Palmer's theory in a way which will suggest to those who have not read his book that it contains extravagant theories, instead of being remarkable for good sense and even knife-like discriminations. But seeing eye to eye with him at so many points, I want him to admit that he has overstated his theory, and that he would accept as the description of the kind of scenery appropriate to poetic drama that it should be unobstrusive and beautiful with a beauty consonant with the spirit of the play performed.

All producers are agreed that it should be beautiful; where they differ is in what they consider to be consonant beauty. Sir Herbert Tree considers any picture which may be called up by the poetry (just as the empty beach rose in my mind while copying the quotation from Titania's speech) to be relevant provided that it can be reconciled with the stage directions; and even if it cannot be, he often puts it in. I remember in his *Antony and Cleopatra* in the middle of the play the lights went down, and as if there was not enough witchery and mystery in Cleopatra herself, a symbolic transformation scene was introduced; a sphinx loomed out of the darkness to die into it again, while, a thrumming, vibrating, aromatic kind of music fell on our ears, to suggest the maddened luxury of the East and the exasperating, enigmatic attraction of the queen. This tableau was greeted, I remember, with louder applause than any part of the play. The scenery at His Majesty's is sometimes charming and beautiful, but, as everybody has been saying for years, amazing, amusing as the scenic effects often are, Shakespeare on that stage is smothered in scenery.

To Mr Poel it is the atmosphere of the Elizabethan playhouse which is always relevant whatever the time and place at which the action nominally takes place. He has taught us much. The beauty and spirit of Shakespeare's age, at any rate, does seem the right inspiration for the consonant setting of some of the plays, but not, I think, of all. Parts of Mr Granville Barker's *Twelfth Night* must have convinced people of this. Mr Gordon Craig often writes as though his chief difficulty would be not to

find decorations and schemes of movement which would produce an effect of beauty consonant with a play, but a play which
would prove duly subordinate to them. Dr Reinhardt (but I
have only seen two of his productions and am generalising
chiefly from his *Oedipus*) seems to hold that if only an effect is
impressive and beautiful it cannot be too strong. He dismisses,
it seems to me, the principle of consonance and subordination
as flimsy and unimportant compared with producing a vivid
effect to the eye. He, too, tethers our imaginations like Sir
Herbert. Mr Granville Barker—but I am to criticise him in
detail next week. I could not do it without explaining from what
point of view I approached *The Midsummer Night's Dream*—
namely, that the setting of poetic drama should be beautiful but
not compete with it, lead our fancies in the direction of the
spirit of the scene but leave them free.

Last week I wrote about the art of producing poetic drama. The
reaping machine went clattering round and round, diminishing
with each circuit the standing corn till it was a mere island in a
shaven field, and when the game did come out, it was only a
small rabbit. The only generalisation which bolted at last was
that the setting of such plays should be beautiful yet undistract-
ing, leading our fancies in the direction of the spirit of each
scene, yet leaving them free.

Had space permitted, I should have gone on to say of the
performance of *A Midsummer's Night's Dream* that I did not
think Mr Norman Wilkinson's scenery beautiful, that it was
distracting and not in harmony with the spirit of the play. I
should have left it at that. I am glad I had no room. I am glad
I had the sense to go again before writing my criticism. I
strongly recommend everyone who, while enjoying the performance, felt dissatisfied with it on such general grounds to go
again. They will enjoy it a great deal more the second time. The
merits of this production come out clearer when surprise at the
scenic effects, the golden fairies, and the red-puppet-box Puck
has subsided.

Mr. Granville Barker has said in his preface that he wished people were not so easily startled. If you are among such people you ought certainly to go twice. The producer has always two choices open to him in such cases. He can employ methods which disconcert at first sight, but when familiar serve his purpose best, or others, not in the end so serviceable, which on first acquaintance are not so likely to attract disproportionate attention. Mr Granville Barker chose the first alternative. I am sure (the newspaper criticisms confirm this) that the majority of the audience thought as much about scenery at the Savoy Theatre as ever did an audience at His Majesty's. It was a different kind of scenery, but just as distracting to most people.

When, however, your astonishment at the ormolu fairies, looking as though they had been detached from some fantastic, bristling old clock, no longer distracts, you will perceive that the very characteristics which made them at first so outlandishly arresting now contribute to making them inconspicuous. They group themselves motionless about the stage, and the lovers move past and between them as casually as though they were stocks or stones. It is without effort we believe these quaintly gorgeous metallic creatures are invisible to human eyes. They, therefore, possess the most important quality of all from the point of view of the story and the action of the play. Dramatically, they are the most convincing fairies yet seen upon the stage. Whether their make-up is the best for making the peculiar poetry of Shakespeare's fairies felt is another question. Personally, I do not think it is.

In this case, as throughout this production, Mr Granville Barker has chosen to bring out the dramatic quality of the scene before the poetic one. He seems to have said to himself, 'I am staging a work written for the stage. It is my business to look after the drama; the poetry can look after itself'. The production is primarily a dramatist's production, not a poet's. You may be thinking, remembering the stuff out of which the play is woven, that this implies a condemnation. As a reader I am with you. I have always enjoyed *A Midsummer Night's*

Dream as a poem, not as a play. What is remarkable about Mr Granville Barker's production is that it shows as has never been shown before, how dramatic also passages and scenes are which seem to the reader to be entirely lyrical. This is a very considerable achievement. There are consequent losses, and these were what at first I felt most; on a second visit to the Savoy it was the positive achievement which impressed me.

People are always wondering whether it is true or not that first judgments of others are most trustworthy. First impressions of people often seem to tell one most, and yet one finds one is always going back on them afterwards. The truth is we are often aware of the *temperament* of a person we meet for the first time more acutely than we are afterwards aware of it again; his character, intellect, etc., we judge of far better on closer acquaintance, so that those we liked at first we often cease to like, and vice versa. If a play can be said to have a temperament, and I don't see why it shouldn't, the temperament of Mr Granville Barker's production was not one which attracted me; but on nearer acquaintance, as might be the case with a human being, I began to be immensely impressed by admirable qualities.

I missed poetry at all sorts of points. Puck was a shock to me. I kept staring at Mr Norman Wilkinson's arrangements in green and red and blue and gold and asking myself if each moment were a picture should I like to buy it, and answering emphatically, 'No'. The scene upon the stage was so absorbing that I did not think of it as a background for acting, and judged it solely on its own merits. But the second.time I was not so attentive to it, and began to notice instead that it served excellently as a generalised background against which any sort of figure, Greek, gilded or bucolic, was more or less congruous. I had ceased to wonder if there were too many silver stars on the curtain of night, or if they were cunningly placed.

I had given up my Puck, a phantom born of reading, a bundle of glorious inconsistencies, and began to wonder, since he must be materialised on the stage, if Mr Calthrop were quite so impossible. Puck is at once will-o'-the-wisp, Oberon's jester, and a rowdy imp; he touches Nature on one side, and on the other country superstitions about poltergeists. Mr Granville Barker has decided, with that peremptoriness which is responsible at once for the merits and the shortcomings of the whole production, that he must be either one or the other, and he has made him a buffoon-sprite. There is nothing of Nature in him, nothing of Ariel, nothing of Loki; he is a clowning bogey. Much of the poetry of Puck is therefore lost. When Puck says, 'I'll put a girdle round the earth in a minute', Mr Calthrop (quite consistently) pronounces these words as a piece of fantastic bombast, and off he struts extravagantly kicking out his feet in a comic swagger. It is true that Puck is a creation of English folklore, but he is English folk-lore transmuted by Shakespeare's imagination, and by turning him again into Robin Goodfellow we lose the effects of that wonderful alchemy. On the other hand all in Puck that is represented in his exclamation 'Lord, what fools these mortals be!' that is to say, all that tells dramatically in such situations as the quarrel between Hermia and Helena and the rivalry between the two lovers, was excellently brought out. Whenever the presence of Puck as a spirit of unmalevolent mischief on the scene adds to the piquancy of the situation Mr Calthrop succeeds. He was very good in this scene, and it was also one of the very best in the performance.

Hermia and Helena (Miss Cowie and Miss Lillah McCarthy) were admirable. Hermia's vindictive, suspicious fury, her gradual transformation into a spiteful little vixen, and the fluttering, frightened indignation of Helena were excellent. The acting revealed more dramatic comedy in the situation than any reader, however imaginative, is likely to feel in it.

Everyone has praised Bottom and his friends. The fussy, nervous, accommodating Quince, the exuberant Bottom, poor timid old Starveling, Snout with his yokel's grin, and Flute with the meek blankness which marks him out for the lady's part, the laconic and cautious Snug—they were perfect.

The performance of Pyramus and Thisbe was the great success of the production; for the first time the presence of an audience, of Theseus and his court, on the stage was a sounding-board for fun. Mr Dennis Neilson-Terry was a graceful and dignified Oberon. His movements, his stillness were delightful to watch. In some passages his elocution was excellent, but his voice—a fine one in timbre—is not yet completely under his control. He fails when the passage demands rapidity of utterance (just, by the by, where Miss McCarthy as a speaker succeeds most), and there is a curious kind of expression of composed surprise in his voice which often suits the lines ill and becomes monotonous. Miss Silver was a delicious Titania. She spoke her first long speech beautifully, or rather the first part of it, losing her art, it seemed to me, over the description of the floods and frosts, recovering it again in her second speech—and delivering perfectly the lines at the close:

> But she, being mortal, of that boy did die;
> And for her sake do I rear up that boy,
> And for her sake I will not part with him.

HAMLET

THE NEW HAMLET

1925

HAMLET IS A PART in which it is very difficult to triumph and easy to avoid complete failure. The character is woven of so many strands that it is capable of various readings; hence its perennial attraction to actors interested in their art. The play itself, too, has different threads of interest running through it, and being too long in its perfect folio form for representation, it has to be cut.

Modern stage versions ignore the story and concentrate upon the character of Hamlet.

Mr. John Barrymore's first night was a formidable ordeal for him. He struck me as a sympathetic personality, not a dominating one, and only to an actor with a dominating personality are such occasions spurs. Some of the best points in his performance confirmed that impression. It was in the passages of friendly tenderness and in those moods when Hamlet feels most the lack of sympathy that he excelled. Excellently as he spoke Hamlet's speech of almost feminine effusiveness to Horatio,

> Since my dear soul was mistress of her choice
> And could of men distinguish, her election
> Hath seal'd thee for herself,

it was still more his manner of breaking off with half-reluctant shyness—'Something too much of this'—that showed most clearly the kind of moments at which his temperament would never fail him on the stage. Though he moved with graceful agility, in retrospect I see him at his best when seated; seated, and fingering his 'inky cloak' while the King and Queen endeavour to persuade him to put off that all-too-pointed mourning; seated alone upon the stage and falling into the famous meditation upon suicide ('To be, or not to be', he delivered well, except for one gust of unnecessary emphasis at the words 'bare bodkin'); seated beside Ophelia's grave, with Yorick's skull between his hands, and speaking perfectly with measured and quaint melancholy the great prose passage, only failing to render as perfectly the flight of bitter philosophic fantasy which breaks it off.

> Imperious Caesar, dead and turned to clay,
> Might stop a hole to keep the wind away, &c.,

should not, to my mind's ear, be spoken ruthfully but wildly and with excited gaiety. Indeed, where Mr Barrymore's interpretation failed was in conveying Hamlet's bitter-gay, intellectual exhilaration, which is the desperate reaction of a thinking sensitive nature against life's humiliations and the depravity of man. Hamlet's neurotic condition—another note in the complicated chord of his character—he did strike. Indeed, in Hamlet's relation to his mother he struck it too hard, so that the scene between Hamlet and his mother took on a Freudian significance. This is a mistake and artistically uninteresting. Hamlet's habit of dwelling in words of hideous emphasis on what most revolts him in his mother's marriage is only part of that general morbid horror of procreation and the physical side of life, which shows so harshly in his treatment of Ophelia, and in the passages (cut in this performance) in which Hamlet jests about the body of Polonius. To turn, therefore, in that scene with his mother, the green light of the Ghost upon Hamlet's face before it appears, to hold her frantically embraced, to speak as during a neurotic trance the lines:

> Nay, but to live
> In the rank sweat of an enseamèd bed,
> Stew'd in corruption, honeying and making love
> Over the nasty sty,

is to degrade the scene ('Angels and ministers of grace defend us') into a psycho-analytic demonstration and even to suggest

that 'the Ghost' is after all a projection of an 'Oedipus complex!'
Mr Barrymore acted it with marvellous energy, but this emphasis is wrong, artistically wrong. Hamlet's behaviour must be
distracted to the last degree, but I see no justification for the
clutching, frantic physical tenderness which Mr Barrymore
exhibits towards his mother. In the first quarto (every actor
should consult the quartos for lights upon Shakespearean parts)
the Queen, in giving an account of it, says: 'He throws and
tosses me about.' Ruthless harshness must predominate and
Hamlet as 'scourge and minister' should not, weeping, hug his
mother in his arms. It is true that the interest of Hamlet's
character depends on 'that within which passeth show', and
though morbid psychology is part of what is within, Hamlet's
'noble mind', should engage far more attention.

One little gesture of Mr Barrymore's in the scene with
Ophelia showed how inclined he was to lose sight of the intellectual Hamlet. When he spoke those words of self-disgust,
'What should such fellows as I do crawling between earth and
heaven', he paused after the word 'earth', and, by surrounding
Ophelia's face with his hands and lowering his voice to a tone
of longing tenderness, conveyed that *she* was 'Heaven'. This
was to narrow the scope of Hamlet's tragic sense of life, re-
peatedly expressed in passionate soliloquies.

I have never seen a Hamlet who played this scene with
Ophelia as it acts itself in the theatre of the attentive reader's
mind. 'Love! his affections do not that way tend', exclaims the
King, emerging from concealment. He would never have said
that had he been spying on our stage-Hamlets. Tree used to
return to kiss the tresses of the prostrate Ophelia; Kean, it is
said, used to play the scene as though Hamlet were counter-
feiting brutality in order to conceal the tenderest passion;
Wilkes, so Davis says, 'preserved the feelings of a liver and
the delicacy of a gentleman'. Mr Barrymore let his voice tremble
to a sob, when he told Ophelia that 'he did love her once'. It
may be traditional, but it is a bad tradition; Hamlet was no
lover. Polonius was nearer the truth when he warned his

daughter that the Prince's vows were 'springes to catch wood-cocks', than he was when he exclaimed 'this is the very ecstasy of love!' Hamlet's outranting of Laertes by the grave is not the expression of passionate love-grief. It is an outburst of hysterical fury in a man suffering, for a hundred reasons, at the sight of an histrionic display of grief in another. He apologizes for that outburst later: 'I'll court his favours,' he says, 'but, sure, the bravery of his grief did put me in a towering passion.' How poor, too, and trite is Hamlet's love-letter to Ophelia compared with his devotion to Horatio! Hamlet was no lover.

An actor could find a clue for playing the Ophelia-scene by recalling Byron's last letter to Caroline Lamb; rage to have done with it, suspicion that she is on the side of his enemies, resentment that life, which had already laid intolerable burdens on him, has also now involved him in 'an affair' from which he cannot extricate himself—O cursed spite!—without inflicting torture and self-reproach. Self-reproach is there, even remorse; but it is the kind of remorse which quickly turns to railing, finding relief from itself in lashing 'woman'. There is a great deal of Byron in Hamlet, or, if you like, of Hamlet in Byron. Stupendous creation as the character of Hamlet is, we must not forget that it follows closely a conventional contemporary pattern, even down to dress and mannerisms. Hamlet is 'The Melancholy Man', whom Sir Thomas Overbury has described in his *Characters*, who appears as Lord Dowsecer in Chapman's *A Humerous Day's Mirth*, as Hieronimo in *The Spanish Tragedy* and elsewhere. He was a Byronic type. 'The Melancholy Man' was a cultured, aristocratic pessimist, castigating the vanities and vices of men, brooding, self-critical, excitable, weak, above all ostentatious of his difference from other men and proud to feel an exile on his earth. It is a mistake to assume that Hamlet's way of looking at things is only the result of his father's death and his mother's marriage; he was by nature 'The Melancholy Man', or, as the nineteenth century would have called him, 'The Byronic Man'.

In this scene, it is the pathos of Ophelia which should hold the stage, and the error of all 'Hamlets' has been to draw our sympathies towards 'the lover'. Do they want pathos? Is there not more in the pain of a girl, uneasy at being used for a purpose she does not understand—perhaps to the danger of the man she loves, meeting him with the trifles in her hands which he had given her? 'I gave you nothing', he growls, twinged intolerably at the sight of those reminders of a tenderness now incredible. How much more moving (the scene being played up to Ophelia) it would be if, instead of sobbing out the words, 'I did love thee once', Hamlet stood glowering at her pretty face, as he uttered them, nodding his head in gloomy recognition of a now incomprehensible fact. An embrace, a sob, destroys her reply, so profoundly touching in its truth and simplicity: 'Indeed, my lord, you made me believe so.' Again, how much more credible such acting would make Hamlet's immediate rush of self-reproach, 'We are arrant knaves all; believe none of us. Go to a nunnery', which in its turn leads on to that torrent of abuse of feminine charm that betrays men into false positions: 'You jig, you amble, you lisp and make wantonness your ignorance . . . Go to, I'll no more on't; it hath made me mad. I say, we will have no more marriages . . . To a nunnery go.' Yet our actors play this scene as though it were a lovers' quarrel! One which might end by Ophelia saying soothingly, 'Darling, you *know* you love me!'

The 'Play Scene' was injudiciously cut and inappropriately the climax of emotion had risen higher on the fall of the curtain in the Act before. True,

> The play's the thing
> Wherein I'll catch the conscience of the King,

is a splendid curtain, but damn curtains. Whatever passion Hamlet throws into these words, he must keep his top note of triumphant excitement for wild snatches of song which burst from him, when the King has rushed from the hall and the torches are tossing; for that whirl of nonsense, irony, joy, which suddenly subsides on the entrance of the quaking Rosencrantz and Guildenstern with the message that the Queen is in great affliction and must see her son.

In the soliloquy in which Hamlet decides not to kill the King while he is praying, no actor has probably excelled Mr Barrymore. It would certainly be hard to do so. His fault as an elocutionist is not to distinguish sufficiently between the verse and the prose passages of his part, and occasionally to underline certain words unnecessarily, as thus:

> There are more things in Heaven and earth, Horatio,
> Than are—*dreamt of*—in our philosophy.

But his delivery was beautifully free from mouthing emphasis; his voice, at grave moments, most gracious and pleasant; his enunciation and phrasing excellently distinct. Every word he spoke (this is rare) was intelligible. Probably no English actor, now that Forbes Robertson has retired, could give us as good a performance.

With regard to the other parts; the King wants careful playing. One hint taken might make all the difference to Mr Malcolm Kean's performance. Though we are meant to think the King a worthless blackguard, it is not until he plots Hamlet's death that his words and actions betray him. On the contrary his speeches to Hamlet are marked by dignified and courteous forbearance, to the Queen never verbally ignoble, and his courage when he faces alone the furious Laertes and the rebels is impressive. The clue to playing the part lies in the note Hamlet scribbles in his book, 'That one may smile and smile and be a villain'; in the King's manner towards Hamlet there should therefore be visible a dubious over-civility, and towards the Queen a rather greasy over-attentiveness. The Ghost I liked, though several critics have crabbed him. I am sure Mr Thorpe is right in wailing out his lines with ominous monotony in a voice like the wind in a chimney. Rosencrantz and Guildenstern have most of their words taken from them and naturally don't know what to do.

Miss Fay Compton as Ophelia is admirable in the scene in which she describes to her father the young Prince's attentions. She is also as touching in the scene with Hamlet as Mr Barrymore's method of playing it allows; and in the mad-scene she is just what—not, alas, more than—one normally expects. This scene, without a thrill-compelling voice and fantastic grace of gesture, inevitably induces that uncomfortable feeling that we ought to be more moved than we are. It is better therefore kept low in tone; and it would, perhaps, help most Ophelias to enter with a lute to which to sing, as the first quarto stage-direction indicates. Let her madness be quite conventional madness; it is safer. Let her not study as some Ophelia's have been known to do, the gestures and expressions of lunatics.

Ophelia's burial was badly stage-managed. Away with these white nuns! The perfunctoriness of the ceremony shocks Laertes, just as the absence of 'a hatchment o'er his father's bones' had previously intensified the grief of that extremely conventional young man. The corpse of Ophelia ought to be borne in by a few rustics from the fields, and Hamlet and Laertes must jump *into* her grave. The callous, competitive rhetoric of that raving pair only gets its true value if the two of them, in the very act of declamation and flying at each other's throats, are actually trampling the poor body underfoot; and the savagery and horror of that must be reflected in the gestures and cries of the onlookers. They, however, stood like supernumeraries.

It is the great fault of the English stage that on it seldom more than three people act simultaneously. The play-scene also suffered from this national defect.

I shall always remember the contrasting exhilaration of watching the Yiddish players at the Scala last year. There was not one old Rabbi, even at the back of the stage, who was not contorted by passion and distress in the top scene of their Messianic play.

HAMLETS IN GENERAL

1930

BY THE TIME these remarks appear in print the soul of Mr Esmé Percy will have migrated from the body of Hamlet to that of John Tanner, but the performance of *Hamlet* at the Court Theatre was in some respects so interesting that when some day a history of stage Hamlets is written it should not be omitted. The performance at the Court proved one thing: that Mr Gordon Craig's methods of production are extremely efficient even when they are not carried out with the fine aesthetic balance which he could have supplied himself. In so far as the performance was indebted to his principles (I will not say to his conceptions, for the lighting at the Court would have sometimes exasperated him like a parody), it was a distinct improvement upon any *Hamlet* I have seen. There being no changes of scene and only one break, we were able to see and hear much more of the play than is usual.

Everybody who knows anything about stage designs and the recent developments in stage-craft knows that the impulse due to the work of Gordon Craig has been the most pervasive and creative of all modern influences. The most eminent and enterprising designers have nourished their imaginations on his. It will be a matter for astonishment and scorn to posterity that his contemporaries made so little use of him and offered him so few opportunities to carry out himself his own ideas. That he is 'damned good to steal from' has been discovered, yet his methods have been labelled as unpractical even by those who have made use of them, and in spite of the fact that their practical simplicity is an essential part of their beauty.

A massive pillar, beyond it a terrace walk, with two flights of steps leading up to it on each side, one steep and the other turning and broken by a landing, proved all that was necessary. When it came to the grave-digging scene, an open oblong in the floor and out-of-door costumes were sufficient to support the amount of illusion necessary. The solemn passage of the ghost, pursued up the steps to the left by Hamlet and his companions, at first occulted by the pillar, then motionless and erect beside and behind it at the top of the steep flight of steps, was most impressive; though why its speech should have been spoken for it, off the scene by another voice, I did not understand. Again, by occasionally throwing light upon the scene from the auditorium, shadows, sometimes coloured, repeated most effectively the gestures of the actors. The duel and the play scenes were, by another change of light, silhouetted in dense black in the foreground against the illuminated spectators on the stage. Aesthetic discretion was by no means always in control of these devices, but Gordon Craig's principle that by means of simple masses of masonry, the grouping of coloured figures and the shifting of emphasis of light and shadow, drama could be intensified, was fully proved. The results often left much to be desired, but they suggested what might be done. Moments of complete darkness marked changes of scene as effectively as a dropping curtain, and changes of light prepared the spectator, by isolating Hamlet in the imagination, for some of the chief soliloquies. The total effect of these devices was to make the performance an excitingly rapid one; *Hamlet* became a play of lurid action.

Hamlet himself was a contrast to this effect. Mr Esmé Percy was admirable in the scene between Hamlet and his mother, and in those moments of urgent conference with Horatio and Marcellus. His fine eyes are noticeable at moments of emotion and his face and gestures can express deep nervous agitation. His carriage and figure, however, lack dignity. His Hamlet belonged to the class of morbid Hamlets; though never mawkish, he was not a Hamlet to whom a funeral with military honours seemed at all appropriate. He was a somewhat feminine Hamlet. It was noticeable that his interpretation toned down ringing lines and the rhetorical rhymed flourishes of the exits. It was characteristic of his performance that he spoke the lines.

E

The time is out of joint: O cursed spite,
That ever I was born to set it right!

with depressed weariness, mounting heavily the steep staircase.
He was inclined to turn the fantastic meditations upon Yorick's
skull into demonstrations of personal grief, which is surely
wrong. The imaginative and intellectual detachment of Hamlet
was thus in part lost, or muted into a temperamental lassitude.
On the other hand, there was often a charming urgency of
tenderness in his address, and often a pathetic ferocity in his
energetic moments fascinating to watch.

It was a happy thought to play the King as a man in the full
flower of life, and the Queen as one whom the King might desire
herself as much as a throne. I never saw the Queen occupy more
easily, yet unobtrusively, her right place in the play than Miss
Miriam Lewis succeeded in doing. Ophelia was not crazy
enough in her main scene, but charmingly demure in the earlier
ones. She went mad in black, not in the traditional white, and
proffered imaginary flowers.

What remains with me from this performance is above all an
impression of hurried, crowded action; and I found that refreshing. Indeed, if the corpse-strewn scene at the end is not
to fail of its effect, this sense of events racing to one overwhelming, comprehensive catastrophe, must be conveyed.

Shakespeare-lore is so bewildering a subject for investigation
that I have made but faint attempts to learn. It is a region of
controversy which it is hardly worth while only to visit; you
must settle down in it to learn anything—and if you do, you are
apt to go mad. The tourist, on entering it, is at once button-
holed by voluble guides, each of whom has apparently good
credentials. But presently, having chosen one, in spite of the
reassuring letters on his cap, the tourist is apt to grow uneasy
on catching from time to time the fixed stare in his guide's eye.
Can he be quite sane? he asks himself, ever with more and
more misgiving. These guides can be divided roughly into four
classes. Those who think Shakespeare wrote not only the plays
attributed to him, but everybody else's; those who think he

wrote only mere fragments of the plays which pass as his, the guide selecting lines he thinks best; those who think that every possible meaning or shade of significance in the works was intentional, and those guides (they are robust fellows) who think that every sublety or meaning beyond that which could have been grasped by the groundlings is pure accident. If the inquirer listens to all he is distracted by bewilderment, and if he listens only to one sort he becomes a monomaniac. I do not recommend Shakespearean studies.

Last time I ventured into those regions I came across a guide of the robuster sort. He pointed out an interesting fact in the history of Hamlet as reflected in opinion down the ages. His name was Dr Elmer Stoll and his pamphlets are published by the University of Minnesota. He showed that our interpretation of Hamlet's character as one sicklied o'er with thought, of the part as a profound study in irresolution and a diseased will, never entered the heads of any one who saw the play till the Romantic Movement was in full swing at the end of the eighteenth century. To all earlier commentators Hamlet was a hero of brilliant dash in a story of revenge, courageous and resolute, who set about the slaying of his uncle as expeditely as the exigencies of the plot, the old plot, allowed. He told me to rub my eyes and read the play again. Look! this is an impetuous, fiery fellow with plenty of self-confidence. His self-reproaches in soliloquy are not judgments on his character but expressions of moods. They find no echo in the judgments passed upon him by Horatio or any other character in the play. They are traditional elements in the drama of revenge. Does not the bloody and impetuous Hieronimo, Hamlet's forebear, indulge in such damaging reflections ? Does not Seneca's Atreus, in the *Thyestes*, brood over his remissness:

O Soul so sluggish, spiritless and weak ?

And do not Medea and Clytemnestra, who have never been considered weak women, spur themselves on by similar self-castigations ? 'Why,' cries Clytemnestra:

Why, sluggish soul, dost thou safe counsel seek,
Why hesitate?

'In these cases,' says Dr. Stoll, 'to be sure, there is no such long interval of delay as in *Hamlet*; but delay of some sort there is in all classical and Renaissance revenge tragedies, and these exhortations serve to motive it.'

In short, we of later days have read our sensitive bewilderments into a character which his creator designed more simply. Well, even if Shakespeare would himself agree with Dr Stoll, we ought to be thankful that we can read in a richer significance.

Figures of literature and history live in the thoughts of men on the condition that they change their aspect. Humanity is only interested in past ages and dead authors in so far as it can attribute to them its own passions and thoughts. That they are able to go on doing so—seeing now this, now that, in them—is the sign and proof of an immortal creation.

OTHELLO

1921

I HAVE BEEN READING Tolstoy on Shakespeare. Nearly all his criticisms are well founded, yet his conclusion is hopelessly wrong. When Tolstoy says that Shakespeare spoilt the old story about the Moor, who murdered his innocent wife from jealousy, what he says is part true, and, oddly enough, though in a very different spirit, Swinburne agrees with him.

Tolstoy says that Iago in Cinthio's story is an intelligible character, while Shakespeare's Iago is quite unreal. He says that in the old romance there is a simple clear motive behind Iago's machinations, for his passion for Desdemona turned to hatred when she repulsed him and preferred the Moor. In this story, Iago steals the handkerchief, and Cassio, finding it in his room and knowing it to be Desdemona's, tries to return it, but, meeting with Othello, he runs away, thereby confirming more naturally and forcibly the suspicions which Iago has already sown in Othello's mind.

Swinburne recognises that the dropping of the fatal hanker-chief and Emilia's, 'I am glad I have found this napkin', are devices less moving and impressive than the contrivance by which Cinthio makes it fall into Iago's hands. In the old story, Iago had a little girl of whom Desdemona was very fond, and once, while she had taken the child upon her lap, the villain twitched it from her girdle. 'No reader of this terribly beautiful passage can fail to ask himself why Shakespeare forbore to make use of it. The substituted incident is as much less probable as it is less tragic.' But, of course, Swinburne finds an explanation: 'There is but one; but it is all-sufficient. In Shakespeare's world, as in Nature's, it is impossible that monsters should propagate: that Iago should beget, or that Goneril or Regan should bring forth.'

This is a good example of the spirit in which the most famous

critics have explained away the blemishes they could not but
see in Shakespeare's work, and Coleridge's praise of Iago's
speech, in which he expounds his intentions, as 'the motive
hunting of motiveless malignity', is another, though a less
glaring example, of the same infatuated determination to see
perfection in carelessness, and subtle profundities in plain
contradictions, where the work of the master poet, the en-
chanter, is concerned. Yet who doubts that Swinburne's estimate of Shakespeare, though he praises him as though he were
a god and not a man, is nearer truth than Tolstoy's ?

Tolstoy thought the world was under a gross delusion with
regard to Shakespeare, because he judged him from the point
of view of a realistic, religious writer, from which he rightly
found Shakespeare's plots and characters full of inconsistencies
and improbabilities and often far from lifelike. He constantly
complains of the bombastic, inflated, affected language in
which all the characters express themselves. Would a man, he
asks, suffering from grief and remorse and intending to kill
himself, make phrases about his services and pearls, and about
his eyes dropping tears 'as fast as the Arabian trees their medi-
cinal gum'? It is absurd and disgustingly unnatural. Tolstoy
has not felt the magic of Shakespeare's marvellous language;
that is to say, he has missed his essential quality. On the level
from which he judges him the faults he finds are usually there,
though reaction against Shakespeare's reputation sometimes
makes him, even on the level of psychology, unfair to him; but
his book is a wholesome corrective to critics who are swept
away by the beauty of poetry into attributing to Shakespeare all
the merits a realistic writer can possess.

If a critic proceeds to assert that Shakespeare's character-
drawing is always true, subtle and profound, Tolstoy has him
on the hip; and if Shakespearean actors act their parts as though
the poetry were not the very soul of the play, their performance,
unless seen with eyes blinded by prejudice, will not be the
exhibition of a world's masterpiece. If the poetry of *Othello*
is not felt, the play becomes an energetic, brutal, rather sense-

less melodrama, open to the most damaging criticism. All that we are then aware of, thanks to having read the play, is that behind the horrors and improbabilities something very wonderful and strange is going on.

The performance of *Othello* at the Court Theatre does not achieve much more than that. I found myself continually criticising it from the realistic level. One reason why Shakespeare is so hard to act, is that up to a certain point parts like Othello and Iago and Desdemona are actor-proof. They cannot fail to make some kind of vivid impression, though that impression may not be aesthetically or intellectually worth much. The advantage of Mr Poel's archaeological method of Shakespearean production is that it prevents the spectator taking the realistic point of view, and leaves the poetry a fairer field. There are other even better ways of achieving this. The fundamental objection to the performance at the Court is that it does not attempt them.

On the realistic plane *Othello* is not over-acted but it is underfelt. Mr Godfrey Tearle has dignity, and he has presence, but he does not communicate passion. His facial expression and pose are often excellent, especially in those passages when Othello is beginning to be uneasy. Miss Madge Titheradge's Desdemona is colourless, painstaking and merely meek; her acting falls as short of real pathos as Othello's does of real passion; Mr Basil Rathbone's Iago inclines to the cat-like, wicked-grinning, demon-detective tradition; Mr Cowley's Roderigo is too much the gaby. Roderigo is a tragi-comic figure; the comedy of the scenes between him and Iago is more delicate than appeared at the Court Theatre. Roderigo is an ass, but he should be an ass with the carriage of a *galantuomo*, a man with a show of martial impetuosity which, it is true, it is easy to dash or divert. Mr Cowley plays him as a yokel with a modest poke and hanging underlip, whom no one could imagine so hot in pursuit of Desdemona that he is prepared to sell all he has and attempt murder to get her. Mr Cellier plays Cassio without finish. A half-articulate, but most sensitive, baffled loyalty is the essence of the part.

Cassio, the friend, is even more pained at losing Othello's trust and friendship than his post; here lies the strength of his appeal to Desdemona. His ruling passion is the one human passion of which Iago, with all his insight into human nature, has no inkling; the desire to serve where he loves and serve disinterestedly. These are the points to bring out. In Cassio, Othello had precisely the kind of friend he *thought* he had in Iago; that is to say, a man in whose affection and honest intentions he could for ever trust. In this Othello and Cassio were alike, that in friendship both were unsuspicious. But where woman is concerned, to say that Othello was not a jealous man is fantastic. Yet critics as fine as Coleridge have said it. Coleridge indeed, denies that Othello killed Desdemona in jealousy. He accepts Desdemona's word that such a passion was contrary to Othello's nature, and Othello's description of himself as 'one not easily jealous, but being wrought, perplexed in the extreme', as true statements, and he proceeds to contrast Othello with Leontes and Pòsthumus, both frank studies in the green-eyed passion. As a matter of fact, Othello himself is entirely mastered by it, and, as Mr Frank Harris points out, being jealous, he is, like Leontes and Posthumus, nothing if not sensual. He is driven to the verge of madness by it, and Iago's words which call up an image of Desdemona in the arms of Cassio throw him into a fit. (The fit was omitted at the Court, perhaps wisely, for Mr Tearle, while he was excellent when Othello was master of himself, and a dignified soldier, could not forget himself in fury, let alone work up to that convulsive climax.) The greater part of the play, indeed, is the exhibition of the frenzies of jealousy. Othello, when he examines Desdemona's hand, and comments on its moist warmth, is seething with the rage of a Leontes at 'paddling palms and pinching fingers'. His exclamations, 'Damn her, lewd minx, O damn her!' and that wonderful

> O thou weed
> Who art so lovely fair, and smell'st so sweet

> That the sense aches at thee—would thou hadst
> never been born

are more revealing of his temperament than the lines:

> It is the cause, it is the cause, my soul.

And:

> Yet she must die, else she'll betray more men.

One need not be an Iago to see in those lines the working of passion to find a moral justification for itself. Had his agony throughout the play been that of the judge who finds he must condemn his dearest, would he have been so blind? One has only to put the question to one's self to see how absurd it is to deny that Othello is consumed with that most extreme jealousy which has its roots in the body.

Of the two sides of Othello's character there is no doubt which Mr Tearle did best. He had not savagery enough for the fiery sensual Moorish side. When he struck Desdemona in the face you felt no thrill of horror. There are some passages within his compass the delivery of which a little care would improve. Mr Tearle spoke the lines:

> Excellent wretch. . . .
> And when I love thee not—chaos is come again

as though he were saying, 'When I cease to love you the end of the world will have come', instead of speaking them as though they were the expression of the agonised confusion of his spirit when he hates her. The line should be broken by a desperate gesture. There should be a radiant impulsiveness too in his manner when he greets Desdemona on landing in Cyprus after the storm:

> O my soul's joy!
> If after every tempest came such calms,
> May the winds blow till they have wakened death!
> . . . If it were now to die,
> 'Twere now to be most happy.

This is the first deep glimpse we get into Othello's vehement, emotional nature. Mr Tearle was too aloof and calm here. It is extremely difficult to retain a musical quality of voice when delivering tirades of overwhelming passion. To say that Mr Tearl failed in this is merely to say that he is not one of the most gifted Shakespearean actors of all time. His facial expression, which was admirable while Iago was dropping his poison in his ear, was not terrible enough when he stood in the last scene beside the curtain of Desdemona's bed, and his voice should sound more ominous when he asks her if she has said her prayers.

As for the cuts (they are always regrettable, except the scene between Desdemona and the clown, which can well be spared), there were only two which were serious mistakes—granted that the culmination of Othello's fury was wisely left unattempted—namely, Iago's soliloquy, which explains his motive for murdering Roderigo, and the omission of Shakespeare's ending, which informs us of what is in store for Iago. His last words:

> Demand me nothing: what you know, you know:
> From this time forth I never will speak word

should make an impression of dauntless contempt and will, against which torture is futile. Mr Rathbone did not deliver them so as to convince us that they were indeed the last words that Iago would ever speak. Shakespeare founded the character of Iago on Cinthio's description of him as 'who had the wickedest nature that ever man had in the world'. He is not a real figure except in a poetic world, and therefore almost impossible to act realistically. In that world he is tremendous. Perhaps the best compromise in such a performance as we see at the Court Theatre would be to represent him as a bluff Bismarckian type. It was inconceivable that anyone should call Mr Rathbone 'honest Iago'.

CONTINENTAL DRAMATISTS

IBSEN AND THE TRAGIC SENSE

1921

JOHN GABRIEL BORKMAN has given place to *Prunella* at Everyman's Theatre, Hampstead. It is to be hoped, however, that it has gone into their repertory; for, although the acting left much to be desired, there were excellent points about M. Komisarjevsky's production, and Mr Franklin Dyall's Borkman was, in the quiet passages, extremely good. The actors were not up to the tragic intensity of their parts, but it is not surprising that they did not succeed in gripping and hurling across the footlights the huge massive emotions the play contains. The performance was well worth seeing, nevertheless, and if another chance of seeing it occurs do not miss it. At least you will be reminded what great drama is, even if it does appear to put too much strain on its interpreters; you will, at any rate, be reminded that there is such a thing as modern tragedy.

Reflecting as I walked down the hill on what I had seen, and upon the failure of the actors and actresses to convey that intensity peculiar to characters whose wills are irrevocably set in one direction, without whom tragedy is impossible, I found an excellent excuse for them in the temper of the times. How could they represent those characters? Such emotional obstinacy was incredible! For the times are anti-tragical; 'Pack up your troubles in the old kit-bag and smile, smile, smile', is the most serious modern contribution to the philosophy of the ages, and, though it is by no means to be despised as a practical one, yet the mood which engenders it is one to which tragedy is incomprehensible. Nowadays 'to die hard' is equivalent to doing something absurd; failure to follow at once the line of least resistance, not to treat the past, even if it is but a few weeks old, as though it had never happened, not to forget, when forgetfulness facilitates, what you felt or stood for a month ago, is to be ridiculous.

No one can deny that it is the temper of the times, and it is killing to the tragic sense; indeed, it presupposes that it is already dead.

A criticism of *Gabriel Borkman* appeared in the *Daily Mail*; it was an interesting criticism because it was an entirely honest one. The writer told the story thus: Gabriel Borkman was a fraudulent financier who, after release from prison, lived seven years pacing up and down a gallery upstairs waiting for a deputation to call on him, while his wife, a most unpleasant woman, lived down below. His old love, her sister, came unexpectedly to see him and he went out, caught a chill, and died. His wife wanted his son to redeem the family name, but he preferred to run off with a frisky widow and he did so. The writer concluded from this rotten story that Ibsen as a dramatist was a wash-out. The summary is quite accurate and the conclusion inevitable, if the passions of the characters are dismissed as incredible and therefore uninteresting. If you cannot believe that Borkman had an irresistible vocation, and that he was an imaginative man to whom the imprisoned millions in the mines called incessantly to release them, you can understand neither how dead he was all those years after his fall, nourishing himself in solitude on the dream that one day his fellow-citizens would find his services indispensable, nor can you understand the significance of his awakening to physical death when Ella visits him. The first effect of that interview, of his first reaction to reality after years of dreaming, is to fill him with hope. 'I have been close to the verge of death', he cries. 'But now I have awakened. I have come to myself. A whole life lies before me yet. I can see it awaiting me, radiant and quickening. And you—you shall see it, too.'

'Never dream of life again', answers his wife. 'Lie quiet where you are.' How absurd to one without the tragic sense it seems that this unforgiving wife has never till then, in all those years, spoken to her husband, and that all she lives for should be to raise a 'living monument' upon his grave, in the shape of her son: 'His life shall be so pure and high and bright, that your burrowing in the dark shall be as though it had never been.' The woman is clearly overstrained ... but to make her breakdown persist for seven years! What nonsense, too, Ella talks; because Borkman married her sister for money, she accuses him of having committed 'a crime for which there is no forgiveness!' ... 'What you held dearest in the world you were ready to barter for gain. That is the double crime you have committed. The murder is on your soul and on mine. ... You have done to death all the gladness of life in me.' And at the last when, from the hill where long ago they used to sit together, they look again across the mining country covered now in darkness and snow, and Borkman listens, as he did in his youth, to the call of his imprisoned millions: 'I love you, unborn Treasures yearning for the light', she breaks out again. 'Yes, your love is still down there, John. But here in the light of day, here there was a living warm human heart that throbbed and glowed for you. And this heart you crushed. Oh, worse than that! Ten times worse! You sold it. ... And therefore I prophesy to you, John Gabriel Borkman—you will never enter in triumph into your cold dark kingdom.'

This is clearly not a woman who packed her troubles in the old kit-bag and smiled, smiled, smiled, and in tragic sentiment 'Bear it and grin' is, I maintain, the highest pitch to which modern sensibility will follow the dramatist. Such a play as this obviously overshoots that pitch and to the modern sense falls plumb into the nonsensical. 'Unforgivable sin!' There is no such thing; neither are there irrevocable crashes in life, or words, however passionate, which cannot be quite simply retracted. Pain, of course, remains, but pain is painful, not tragic; besides, even that can be avoided perhaps by repeating, 'I am better and better every day in every way'.

The sense of the momentous and irrevocable is too weak just now for Ibsen to be understood, who in his own fashion was as possessed by it as Robert Browning, Carlyle, or any revivalist He was both realist and poet, but he did not write his best when he wrote only as a realist (*The League of Youth*, *The Pillars of Society*, *The Doll's House*, etc.); though he was always a marvellous craftsman, or when he wrote chiefly as a poet (*Brand, Emperor and Galilean*); his real power showed when from his vision he began to create types, and lastly when in his old age he began to draw his dramas from his inner experience. Where he was unrivalled was in finding a story, just matter of fact enough to be plausible and exactly fitted to carry his thought, which was exciting and profound. Indeed, the intensity of the thought below the current of events was so great, that he could even indulge in concrete and arbitrary symbolism without the story losing its matter-of-fact convincingness. It is not his stories which are so remarkable, but the significance within, and it is with that the present generation is losing touch, for when Ibsen is not hewing at some social evil he is essentially a tragic poet.

Much has been written about the nature of tragedy and why it should delight men; this famous 'purging of the emotions' through the spectacle of suffering—what is meant by it? Art enables us to focus our dumb emotions, and by so doing relieves them. Tragedy does not show that evil is somehow good or calamity a blessing in disguise; to do that is the function of apologetics and dubious theology. It simply confronts us with the apprehension of how evil evils are and what goods are possible though they may be thwarted. It finds expression for sorrow just as other forms of art express joy, and both bring the same relief and gratification through expressing what was previously in us dumb or half-articulate and confronting us with it. Catharsis is not a result peculiar to tragedy. But it can appeal, of course, only to those who in their lives confront sorrow and calamities and do not shuffle them out of sight. The genius of Ibsen at the close of his career was a purely tragic genius; his theme becomes spiritual death, not regeneration. You may say that the public never understood him. They did not, but they felt there was something there to understand. My impression is that they are losing that dim perception, and chiefly because they handle the stuff of tragedy in their own experience differently.

DRAMA AND DOSTOEVSKY

1926

THE PRODUCTION OF *The Idiot* at the Little Theatre is
certainly much more interesting than most plays running
at this moment, but it is also far more disappointing than
all but the poorest of them. It is disappointing because it is
practically impossible to dramatize Dostoevsky, though he is
the most dramatic of all novelists, and because it is very difficult
for English actors and actresses (unless they are trained and
looked after by a producer like M. Komisarjevsky) to act Russian
characters. The moments on the stage when Russian characters
are supposed to be speaking out of themselves are just those
which are apt to appear on our stage particularly unnatural.
Mr Michael Hogan, who adapted the novel and produced the
play, undertook a task of enormous difficulty, probably impossible to achieve with complete success. That he might have done
it better than he did, I also believe. Let what I have to say about
this play be read in the light of that admission.

Dostoevsky's method as a novelist is essentially dramatic; his
characters exhibit themselves in talk—in pages and pages of
dialogue. Compare him with Tolstoy and one notices how little
he relies in comparison on description or statement. Tolstoy
states briefly what is in the minds of his characters; he describes
with unmatched vividness how they look and behave. True, the
people in his stories when they speak always speak in character,
but we get to know them so well largely through *seeing* them
act and move before us. Dostoevsky's method of approach is
the reverse. He gets his effects, not by describing in each case
the body and its gestures so vividly that we divine the movements of the soul, but by making his characters expose so completely every emotion within them in talk that we can infer
their substantiality.

It might seem, then, that the dramatist who aims at putting a
Dostoevsky novel on the stage, has only to choose the passages
of this wonderfully revealing dialogue and string them together.

F

But there is an insuperable difficulty: Dostoevsky's method is expansive. Look at the length of his novels and the short time the action occupies. He requires as many pages to describe the events of hours as Tolstoy takes to describe the events of years. Profusion, intricate modulation, repetition are essential to Dostoevsky's effects. Each drop of water, each minute, is put under a microscope; in the end there is a revelation of swarming life positively oceanic in effect, but the method is one inadaptable to the stage. Only on the Chinese stage, where a play is permitted to last a week or so, could the dramatist hope to produce the same result. Attempts to telescope Dostoevsky's intricate, impassioned conversations inevitably over-emphasise the crude erratic violence of the situations and the spiritual melodrama of these huge stories, which are only made convincing by innumerable strokes—subtle, unexpected and profound. It takes more time than stage-presentation allows to burrow into the characters as deep as Dostoevsky's themes require. We must, also, get gradually used (this is especially true of an English audience) to the hectic, restless chaos in which his characters live, before we can measure their moral natures or estimate the momentum of the emotions impelling them. If this preparation is scamped, the climaxes appear hysterical or lurid.

This was the case on the stage of the Little Theatre, and I do not see how it could have been otherwise. What can we make of Aglaya, if we have heard her only utter a few sentences before her scene with Nastasia and Muishkin? She must seem to us merely a wild hysterical little thing; we may be sorry for her, but she can hardly seem tragic to us. And how much more development is required in the case of Nastasia than the sight of her excited behaviour in Act II, if we are to understand how, in her unselfish adoration of Muishkin was shot with a morbid self-centred impulse towards death and suffering.

The softening, calming influence of Muishkin's saintliness on others, when restricted to a few signal instances, instead of being spread out like a sweetness in the common air, becomes suspiciously evangelical. I thought Mr Ion Swinley's performance no mean one—quite the contrary; yet Muishkin on the stage was not entirely unreminiscent of the principal figure in that sentimentalised drama of the power of goodness, *The Passing of the Third Floor Back*. I think Mr Michael Hogan made a mistake in substituting for the closing scene of the novel, in which Muishkin soothes the raving murderer Rogozin, Rogozin's suicide and an idiot's monologue for Muishkin to speak as the curtain falls. Rogozin was too crazy a figure to be interesting. Mr Michael Hogan, who acted the part, found himself driven to reinforce the interest of the part by physical contortions and grimaces almost as violent as Muishkin's rapidly evanescent fits.

The defects of the stage-version which I have dwelt upon seem to me inevitable, but where the critic may with justice bring Mr Hogan to book, is over the failure of the production to animate the whole of any scene. Too often the figures on the stage were grouped as a *tableau vivant*, while a duologue of impassioned violence was taking place. This inevitably destroyed the intensity of the effect. The dialogue required to be more evenly distributed at such moments, the duologue occasionally broken, and the speaking of the lines better timed. The most perfectly adequate acting was seen in the minor parts; Ferdishemko (a remarkable performance by Mr. Clive Currie, whom I shall look out for in future) and Ivolgin (Mr George Cooke). The best passages were Mr Ion Swinley's acting in the first act and Miss Stella Arbenina as Nastasia, in Act III, Scene I. In Act II she failed to give the impression of wild misery simulating hardness and gaiety. On her entrance, we could not gather what her mood was or what sort of a woman she was; her transitions of emotion appeared merely pathological. But in the last act her pleading resignation was admirable. Aglaya (Miss Beatrix Thomson) acted well, but we had seen too little of Aglaya to be deeply interested in her.

I wish to conclude this notice by saying that although I could only enjoy the play with reservations, it is not waste of time to see it. Nor is it one for which those who care for drama will be ungrateful; it flutters and flops, but it is a brave attempt to fly.

STRINDBERG

THE FATHER

1927

THE TWO MOST important facts about Strindberg, apart from his genius, were that he was liable to violent attacks of suspicion-mania and that he could not get on with or without women and married wife after wife. He did not know how to live with women, or how to quarrel with them, how to make it up, or how to break with them. They threw him into a state of agonized bewilderment shot with flashes of piercing hate-directed insight. A large part of his work may be roughly described as the sorrows of a hen-pecked Blue Beard. Possessing the lucidity of genius, he could also suddenly recollect himself and see himself as mad or impossibly exacting; and he rightly named his longest account of the agonies of such an intimacy *The Confessions of a Fool*. Being a poet, he could sometimes invest such agonies with the tatters of a lurid beauty and make you feel, 'O what a noble mind is here o'er-thrown', but he could never put the personal aspects of exasperation and misery far enough behind him; never get rid of resentment towards the figments of his imagination because of their resemblance to the actual persons who had served him as models. His imagination and his power of reviving as he wrote intense perceptions of what he had experienced enabled him to create figures filled with powerful vitality, but once created he could not let them go their own way or allow them the right to live, however balefully, as human-beings. He would snatch up his own creations and by doing so turn them into wax-effigies to stick with nails of spite and roast before the fire of his private anger. This is clearly to be seen in the play I am about to criticise; and this degrades it from the category of the excellent to that of the remarkable.

The same flaw runs through nearly all his work. (I have not read his historical dramas; perhaps they and his fairy dramas should be excepted.) His art judged as a whole is of the kind often euphemistically called 'cathartic' (unduly exalted in periods of perplexity), in which egotism, sometimes sympathetic. sometimes childish, sprawls and spews before the public, indifferent to the impression it makes so long as it exhibits itself. Strindberg was a struggler: 'To search for God and to find the Devil! That is what has happened to me' he cries in *Inferno*. The man who is all struggle may be huge, but he cannot be great.

The curtain goes up; we are looking into one of those northern homes which give us an odd arresting sense of isolation. This is the study of a distinguished man of science (Strindberg—I never could make out whether, or not, it was one of his delusions—considered that he had made, or was on the verge of making, important mineralogical discoveries), and the owner of the study is also a cavalry captain. As usual, the only neighbours are a pastor and a doctor; and without the home broods the terrific atmospheric pressure of gossip and respectability—quite Ibsenish, in fact. The spirit of the drama is, however, not at all like Ibsen. In Ibsen the woman nearly always has the *beau rôle*; in Strindberg's plays she is not even the conduit of disaster, but evil itself. The house is upside down. 'The Captain' is struggling in a mesh woven by the maleficent wills of wife, nurse, mother-in-law and grandmother-in-law. (Mr Loraine acted admirably throughout the neurotic lion.)

The struggle of the moment is over the education of his daughter; her mother wants to make her an artist on the strength of the admiration of a young man who was rather in love with the girl, her grandmother wants to make her into a spiritualist, the servants to convert her to the Salvation Army, the Captain's old nurse into a Baptist; while he is determined that she shall be taken out of confusion and sent away to school. He will assert his rights as 'the Father'. Her mother is equally determined that she shall control the destiny of her child, and, as we presently see, she is a formidable woman of relentless cunning—all the more formidable because she is entirely without magnanimity or a sense of honour, and because her cunning is of the hand-to-mouth kind.

Ibsen was fond of showing how much more humane women were because they were not conscience-ridden, often too, how much more sensible they were in consequence. Strindberg revelled in showing that it made them monsters. Laura will stick at nothing to get her way. She is prepared, we discover, to drive her already neurotic husband crazy, and in order to hasten that process and detach him from his child, to suggest that he is not her real father. Her method of getting her own way hitherto has been to exasperate him into nerve storms, and to reinforce the impression he makes at such times on others by writing letters, in which she intimates that she fears he is not in his right mind. Their last doctor, however, had seen that he was fundamentally sane, so by making this man's life unbearable in the neighbourhood Laura has got another doctor to take his practice. He, she hopes, may prove more amenable. He does, though he at once catches her out lying about her husband. Lying, did I say? That word gives a false impression of the semi-conscious subtlety of her schemes. Even her crass stupidity, her miscomprehension of her husband's work, helps her towards the end her remorseless will is set upon. She tells the doctor that her husband suffers from delusions. She tells him that he thinks he knows what is going on in the planets from looking through a microscope. The doctor pricks up his ears; but when he talks to 'The Captain' himself he discovers that he is merely investigating the composition of planets through the spectrum. When that piece of information has failed in its effect, Laura is surprised but unperturbed.

In a dispute with her husband she learns, or thinks she learns, that if a child is illegitimate the father has no control over its education. She then proceeds to suggest to him that Bertha is not his child, a suggestion which takes instant and deep root, because in the opening scene we have seen him confronted, as a soldier in authority, with a paternity case he cannot solve. In his already half-distracted state the doubt drives him to real, though temporary, insanity. She then tells the doctor that her husband has an extraordinary delusion that he is not Bertha's father, which is amply confirmed by his ravings upon that point. The doctor is thus won over, and 'The Captain's' old nurse coaxes the exhausted patient into a strait-waistcoat. She hypnotizes him into docility by crooning old nursery reminiscences to him—a terrible scene, excellently acted by Miss Haidée Wright. He struggles, but it is too late to escape, and he finally falls into a state of unconsciousness which may end in death or a living death in a lunatic asylum.

Now, why this horrible woman behaves in this way, and where that flaw I spoke of as running through Strindberg's work comes in, are questions which the reader may well ask. Strindberg puts into her mouth the statement that she detested her husband as a husband, though she was willing to mother him as a sick child, but the dramatist has, without knowing it, drawn the portrait of a man with whom no woman could ever live in peace and affection.

There are two sides to 'The Captain's' nature, both as extreme as they were in Strindberg himself; the impulse of the tyrant, of the gigantic hero whom woman, and especially a wife, must blindly obey, and a soft yielding, pathetic side which cries out to be petted and nursed like a child. The passage from one state to the other is in this case unmodulated by a touch of humour; they are both stark demands upon a wife, who cannot well regard the same man both as a sublime, unshakable hero and as a baby. The interest, however, of this double emotional demand is that in a less violent form it is so common as to be, not perhaps what every woman knows, but, at any rate, recognisable by many an egotistic man, and one which is met, if at all, only by cautious bigamy. The fury and despair of Strindberg at finding that the same woman cannot be an adoring slave, and the next moment (just as his quick moods shift) the patient and tender mother, vented itself in a malignant analysis of 'woman'.

Although it is absolutely necessary dramatically that Laura

should deceive both the doctor and the pastor, Strindberg's rage against her is so hot that he makes, certainly her brother the pastor and in a lesser degree the doctor, actually see through her! It is difficult to recall a more striking nemesis of failing to attain in art the indifferent justice of the artist.

MISS JULIE AND THE PARIAH

1927

A HIGH TEMPERATURE ought not to prevent one appreciating Strindberg; some dramatists, perhaps, but not Strindberg. Yet when, on returning from Play Room Six, 6 New Compton Street (from Cambridge Circus, New Compton Street is the first turning on the right off Charing Cross Road going towards Oxford Street; No. 6 is about thirty yards down on the right-hand side. Play Room Six is on the first floor; it has been entirely redecorated with hycolite liquid wallpaper)—when, as I was saying, on my return, the thermometer told me that, medically speaking, I ought to have been in bed long ago, I was inclined to think that the uncanny uneasiness, the rather unpleasant but interesting uneasiness, I had experienced during the performance must have been due to purely physical causes. This was a disappointment. I had been congratulating myself in some such terms as this: 'Why, after all these years, your sensibilities are still as fresh and unanalysable as a child's; as subtle and unaccountable as those of the extraordinary people who say they can detect the presence of an invisible kitten in a cathedral!'

It is a great thing, of course, for a critic to continue susceptible to impressions he does not understand. The limitations of elderly people in all directions spring from only heeding what they already understand, or think they do. Naturally, therefore, I had been gratified by my evening's experience, and, naturally, I resented the hint of the thermometer. I took it, however, to the extent of ceasing to flatter myself in a general way; but, as the first sentence of this article shows, the conviction remained that, in this case, my peculiar condition had been a help and not a hindrance to me as a critic. You understand *Epipsychidion* best when you are in love; *Don Juan* when anger is subsiding into indifference. Why not Strindberg when you have a temperature?

Let me explain, or rather, try to explain—for I am writing under the influence of fever, which resembles the influence of drink in that, while you grasp the content of each moment, whether that content is one of sensation or reflection, and with unusual vividness, you are also unusually hazy about transitions—let me, then, *try* to explain. My only chance of doing so is to say straight away what idea I am after. If I do not seize it this very moment, it will melt, I know, like a cloud into another, so absorbing that I shall not remember my intention. It is, then, this: that there is an analogy between the sensations of fever and the æsthetic feelings inspired by a Strindberg play; and that these feelings cannot be better described than in terms of such an analogy. To obtain your assent I must remind you of feverish sensations.

It is curious. Your sensations during fever are nearly indistinguishable from pleasant ones, and yet there is a mockery about them all. To have a high temperature is the most splendid (and most unfair) sermon on the vanity of physical pleasures. You are consumed with the most promising thirst; there at your elbow stands the long, cool drink. You drink. What an uncanny and distressing disproportion appears between the glorious magnitude of that craving and the tiny satisfaction it brings! This tired, tender ache which is all over you like a voluptuous feeling seems to promise deepest rest; but the exquisite diminuendo of consciousness does not ensue! This fine sensitiveness to the chill of sheets; how delightful it will be to nestle into glowing warmth! The glow comes. Good heavens! it was not warmth you wanted. Turn the pillow, try the other side—there's a little cool strip left for one leg, at any rate, between the hang-over and the mattress.

Everyone has experienced these feverish sensations. The peculiarity about them, which makes them distressful, is not so much that they are in themselves unpleasant as acutely tantalizing; they are cravings closely associated with deep satisfactions which never follow. One's whole sensuous being is continually concentrated in expectation, and continually cheated. There is no better analogy for the effect on the mind produced by works of genius which are not works of art. Strindberg's plays rouse emotional expectations and leave one thirsty, restless, and either too hot or too cold. The very fact that he possesses what is roughly conveyed by the word 'genius' makes their difference from satisfying work more obvious. They are products of the unfortunate 'cathartic' type of creation, which purges no one but the creator. The keenest form of attention they rouse is curiosity; and that curiosity, when it finds its proper direction, is concentrated upon the author, not on the work. I could see nothing in *Miss Julie* but Strindberg's 'servant' complex (see *The Son of a Servant* passim), his morbid desire to be kicked himself when loved, and the revolt of his masculine pride against that 'complex', taking the form of detestation of the object which satisfies it.

One midsummer night—thus the outline of the story runs—Julie, the only daughter of a Swedish count, bullies her father's footman into taking her to his bedroom; afterwards he has the opportunity of bullying her. They are both thoroughly frightened, and the solution which recommends itself is to lend her the razor, with which he was about to make himself respectable before carrying up his master's boots and coffee, in order that she may cut her throat. Strindberg's temperament has here stepped in and excluded all possibility of our feeling pity for the girl (he would never allow that) consequently the mood in which the fall of the curtain leaves one is: 'Well, well, she cut her throat and her father rang for his breakfast.'

This is hardly a 'catharsis'. It may have relieved Strindberg to send a high-born minx to an ugly death, but in me it inspired what is best described as a state of depressed equanimity. The dramatist's attitude towards the footman (well played by Mr Douglas Burbridge) is rather more difficult to determine. He is certainly innocent in all that preceded their embraces. He behaved like a natural straightforward fellow and told her she was a fool not 'to keep her place', though her tumble from it in a way rejoiced him. But when he took her canary to the kitchen dresser and chopped off its head, I am afraid, remembering the pug, or chow, or whatever it was, in *The Confessions of a Fool*, that the incident was not intended to alienate our sympathies but to illustrate 'the way of a *man* with a maid'. Julie's love of the bird, which she brought down in a cage as her sole luggage when they intended to elope together (I never quite grasped why this solution of their predicament was finally dropped) was, I fear, intended to exemplify the unfathomable falseness of feminine emotion.

There were, of course, vital and remarkable passages in the dialogue. The fact that when Julie falls, she falls, not to her servant's level but below it, was admirably brought out. The naturalness and integrity of his relations to the cook, Christine, who is his mistress, were made an excellent foil to the ugly muddle of his relations with his mistress in the other sense of the term. Of course, 'genius' was there, but—and this is my point—the very vehemence of the author's imagination served to throw into relief the disappointing emptiness and confusion of his conception behind the detail and the dialogue.

Miss Julie was preceded by *The Pariah*. And here I must remark upon the nature of these performances at Play Room Six. You find yourself in a little room in front of a tiny stage; and if you are in the first three or four rows, and the scene is an interior, you feel as though you were in the same room as the actors. This adds intensity to the effect of subtle realism, and makes it practically impossible to bring off stagey effects, even when these would be impressive in a theatre.

The Pariah is a dialogue between two men admirably adapted to performance in these circumstances. They are seated at a bare table with an inkpot on it, in a bare room; the looking-glass over the mantelpiece is at the back of the younger of the two. They have been living together some time (I arrived a little late, so I am not sure of this), and are about to part. The elder (Mr Michael Sherbrook) is studying the other with a detached curiosity which begins to get on the departing friend's nerves. The thunder also fidgets him. Michael Sherbrook (every pucker of his face, every pause in his slow deliberate tones tells) begins by saying that The Other One has puzzled him. 'For instance, you seem to be made up of two men. Looking at your face, you seem a man who braves life, while your back, which I see in that glass, is that of a man cringing under a burden. It is the back of a slave.'

Well, to condense—and necessarily, therefore, to spoil—the dialogue, after slowly piecing together, in a meditative and disconcerting manner, scraps of half-forgotten observation and deductions from The Other One's non-committal replies, the truth emerges: firstly, that this young man has served a term of imprisonment for forgery; secondly, for he has not the air of one who has paid for his misdeeds, that he has also done something else for which he fears, but has not yet received, punishment. Michael Sherbrook tries first to put a little self-respect into him by telling him that he himself killed a man. At this turn of the dialogue I thought that we were in for a robust Nietzschean moral, but the confession turned out to be the most innocent manslaughter. Cringing gratitude in The Other is presently replaced by the snarl of the blackmailer, the malice of the trapped jackal. Conclusion: Out you go, you cur. Thus they parted.

Now, what was the point of this little scene? I was interested because I felt I was in the room with these two men, eavesdropping. But what was the point? There was no point. Strindberg was just working off contempt for a type, very probably identified in his mind with somebody with whom he had been in contact. Again, as always happens when insight is merely hate-directed, the dramatist did not remember that cold and half-amused probing of another's shame does not rouse in the subject the best human response. This revelation of the hopelessness of the Pariah's case was no proof of it. Again: amazingly clever, quite empty.

But how well and quietly Mr Sherbrook acted!

PIRANDELLO

SIX CHARACTERS IN SEARCH OF AN AUTHOR

1922

THE STAGE SOCIETY produced a most original play last Monday and acted it extraordinarily well. The play is by Signor Luigi Pirandello, who is one of the leading Italian dramatists and a writer of admirable short stories. It was produced last year in Rome and made a great impression. The Stage Society's programme included a note by A. W. on the play. It was needed; for without some introduction, many of the audience would have been puzzled by this experiment in dramatic form.

'It is neither a play within a play, not yet a play in the making. Rather it is a trial—possibly an indictment—of the modern theatre. The author has created Six Characters and imagined for them a situation of poignant intensity. And then, doubtful of the theatre's adequacy of his intentions, he abandons his play—it is not to be written. But the characters remain; he has endowed them with life and they refuse to relinquish his gift. A theatrical stock company meets to put another Pirandello play into rehearsal, and as they begin their work, the six characters arrive, and demand that their story shall be given the dramatic representation for which it was destined.'

What an extraordinary plot for a play! How can a play be made out of such a situation? It certainly required considerable cleverness to do it, but Signor Pirandello is clearly endowed with a quite enormous amount of ingenuity. This is how he did it.

The curtain did not go up. It was up when we assembled; we found ourselves sitting in front of the dark empty stage, and presently, one after the other, a number of actors and actresses in their everyday clothes walked on. The humorously-strident voice of Mr Alfred Clark was heard giving directions for a rehearsal, and the lights were turned up. A slightly quarrelsome, snappy chatter followed, and the rehearsal was just getting under way, when at the back of the stage appeared a gloomy procession of figures dressed in deep mourning. An elderly man in immaculate black, a woman, presumably a widow, in streaming weeds, a tiny girl, a young girl about eighteen, a youth, say twenty-two, and a little boy about twelve. These people are 'Characters' in a play Signor Pirandello intended to write.

The rehearsal stops; the actors turn and stare, and Mr Alfred Clark naturally asks the intruders what the devil they want. Diffidently the Father (Mr Franklin Dyall) steps forward. It is quite easy to state why they are come, but not so easy to convince the assembled actors that the visitors are not lunatics. What these protentously grave intruders want is to be given the opportunity of living through the story for which their creator created them. At present they are hanging in a miserable sort of void; they are real—there they are, solid human beings, men and women, boys and girls—but there is nothing for them to do. Politely, but with a certain insistence which gradually mesmerizes the matter-of-fact, dumbfounded Mr Clark (call up the image of a man vigorously, not to say blatantly, matter-of-fact), the Father explains that such a condition of nebulous unattached existence has become intolerable. They *must* fulfil their destiny; would the company kindly impersonate them and thus bring rest to their perturbed spirits ? (No one can act better than Mr Clark that frame of mind which is expressed by the simple words, 'Well I'm blowed!')

Interrupted by the titters of the actors and the passionate corrections of his family, each of whom has his or her version of their terrible story, the Father actually succeeds in getting the idea lodged in the Producer's head that the terrible events through which his family have lived might make a better play than the exceedingly doubtful stuff Signor Pirandello has actually provided. Their story intrigues him.

The Father explains that he married beneath him. 'You see this poor woman ?'

'But she is a widow, and you are alive!'

'Yes, but listen. I married her. I had a secretary; they loved each other; they were continually signalling to each other with their eyes for fear they should wound me by their words; it became intolerable. I let them go off together, and with them went my son—the young man over there.'

Here the Stepdaughter (I have not seen Miss Muriel Pratt act so well before) breaks in with a passionate accusation against the Son, describing his intolerable icy contempt for the rest of the family . . .

Confusion. . . .

The Father resumes his story. He had no idea that, after the death of his wife's lover, the family had fallen into poverty. . . .

More passionate family recriminations. . . .

He had lost sight of them; he is a man not old enough to be indifferent to women and yet too old to be loved by them: a very humiliating condition . . . in short he has recourse occasionally to . . . . well, he buys his loves.

Now, it is very unfair to think that the whole of a man is in all his actions; yet others always judge him as though that were the case. A most terrible thing happened. He went to a certain house which under the pretence of being a dress-maker's was a house where these sort of bargains are struck, and there, without recognizing her, he met his wife's daughter, 'the girl you see over there'. They were interrupted by the cry of the Mother who had come to see her daughter. Imagine how terrible his predicament is now! The girl only sees him in the light of that interview; he is to her merely *that* man. . . .

More interruption from the Stepdaughter, who expresses her loathing and contempt. . . .

Agonized distress on the part of the Mother.

This is the situation which precedes the climax. It rather takes the Producer's fancy, who suggests that the Characters should reproduce what happened before the actors and a shorthand writer. This is just what the characters want, but they are terribly disappointed when they see themselves afterwards impersonated. They come out completely different characters; there is something fatally wrong with the stage version. What we see is the contrast between 'actuality' as an author imagines it and what actually gets across the footlights.

Signor Pirandello has illustrated what every profound dramatist must feel when he sees his characters on the stage; his sufferings at the inevitable distortions due to the substitution of the personality of the actor for that of his character as he imagined it. But he has done more than that. He has suggested the inevitable limitations of the modern drama, the falsifications which result from cramming scenes into acts and tying incidents down to times and places. And he has done more yet; in an odd way he has suggested that the fate of many people is not unlike those of the 'Characters' in the play; that many of us are in their predicament, namely, like them, real enough people, for whom fate nevertheless has not written the plays in which we might have played a part.

Mr Franklin Dyall's performance was of the first excellence; it was difficult to pull it off and he succeeded triumphantly.

CHEKHOV

THE THREE SISTERS

1929

WHENEVER I HAVE occasion to write about Chekhov I always recommend an excellent book of criticism: Mr Gerhardi's *Anton Chekhov*. It deals with the whole of his work, but that part of it concerned with the dramatist ought to be read by everyone interested in modern drama.

'How did he do it?' Mr Gerhardi writes. 'Not by dispensing with plot, but by using a totally different kind of plot, the tissues of which, as in life, lie below the surface of events, and, unobtrusive, shape our destiny. Thus he all but overlooks the event-plot; more, he deliberately lets it be as casual as it is in real life. Before Chekhov realism was no more than a convention. Realistic literature had begun to bear a closer resemblance to real life as it piled on more and more certain superficial irrelevancies characteristic of real life. . . . The object of realistic literature was obviously to resurrect the complete illusion of real life by means of things characteristic of real life, they forgot to make the plot characteristic of real life; so much so that Mr Bennett once confessed that, so far as the story was concerned, the odds were against any novel happening in real life. Chekhov saw that, and made his plots characteristic of real life by choosing for his themes stories which were not of the unlikely kind (because taken from real life and developed into 'stories'), but just as they would probably have happened if allowed to run their natural course in real life.' *The Three Sisters* is a prime example of this art. It is to my mind the best of all his plays.

And there are two other characteristics common to all his plays, most interesting to the critic of modern realistic drama, and from which much can be learnt. First of all—and here, too, I make use of the words of another critic, the late George Calderon, who translated as long ago as 1912 *The Sea-Gull* and

The Cherry Orchard—the interest of Chekhov's plays 'is, so to speak, centrifugal instead of self-centred. . . . They seek, not so much to draw our minds inwards to the consideration of the events they represent, as to cast them outwards to the larger process of the world which those events illuminate; that the sentiments to be aroused by the doings and sufferings of the personages on his stage are not so much hope and fear for their individual fortunes as pity and amusement at the importance which they set on them, and consolation for their particular tragedies in the spectacle of the general comedy of Life in which they are all merged.' (I query the word 'consolation', but let that pass.)

Secondly, Chekhov solved, far better than his contemporaries the problem of naturalistic dialogue, of preserving the triviality and broken rhythms of ordinary talk and still making every word significant of character, and those group relations and larger processes which George Calderon noted. It was easier, or perhaps it only seems easier now Chekhov has done it, for a Russian to write this kind of dialogue—the Russians speak more readily out of themselves than English men and women. Anyhow, he succeeded perfectly in doing for his own people what modern English dramatists have hitherto only approximately accomplished for us. Mr Granville Barker in his two last unacted plays, *The Secret Life* (1923) and *His Majesty* (1928), and in his rewritten but unacted version of *Waste*, has made far the most competent and successful attempt to write dialogue in this way. When *The Secret Life* was published I did not see what he was after—which was a revelation of the inner life through the medium of informal and casual talk such as Chekhov achieved. It is very difficult for the imagination to function while *reading* a play, and mine did not.

Now the kind of acting which is absolutely essential in the case of such plays is acting which restores the unity of impression. The method of this dialogue is disjunctive; the underlying unity must therefore be made prominent, and this can be done only by keeping every actor and actress on the scene con-

tinuously and simultaneously acting. Mr Komisarjevsky's productions of Chekhov are beyond comparison successful because
he insists upon this simultaneity. The result is not confusing.
The dramatist has put words into the mouths of each character
so characteristic that there is no need for the rest to make a space
either of silence or stillness round those who are speaking. The
spectator loses himself completely in the scene before his eyes.
At the Fortune Theatre I only regained consciousness of my own
identity in between the acts. That is the test of a good production of a good play.

The Three Sisters was first performed in London in the spring
of 1920 by the Art Theatre Society: they made rather a hash of
it. It was acted again at Barnes two years ago. This was a fine
performance. Mr Komisarjevsky produced it and several of the
cast were the same as those acting now at the Fortune Theatre.
The part of Solyony is again taken there by Mr Elliot Seabrooke
(he is very good), and Mr Daniel Roe again acts excellently the
old army doctor. I recognized, too, Miss Margaret Swallow as
Masha, Mr Douglas Burbridge as Andrey and Mr Ion Swinley
as Vershinin. All these parts are well acted. I have one fault,
however, to find with Mr Swinley. Vershinin is a one speech
character. Whenever he is moved he breaks out into an impassioned discourse about the glorious future for which the
thwarted petty lives of the present generation are a preparation.
It is largely through his liberal eloquence that he first touches
the heart of Masha. But as time goes on something mechanical
ought to creep into his delivery. His speech ought therefore to
have been more fervid when he was addressing a new audience,
and his last repetition of it, when he is parting from Masha,
would then by contrast have the flatness of a gramophone record;
thus giving another turn to the ironic screw. Andrey is admirable in his seedy, lazy dilapidation which results from his
disastrous marriage to the hard, vulgar, little upstart Natasha. I
was not quite satisfied with Miss Margot Sieveking's interpretation. She ought to have been more odiously self-assertive in
contrast to the helpless refinement of 'the three sisters'. Yet

one realized, while watching those scenes between her and her sisters-in-law, what a handicap magnanimous sensitiveness is in dealing with a sobbing, hectoring, managing vulgarian. Olga seemed to me perfect. There have been dramatists with a wider sweep and a stronger hand than Chekhov, but none has brought to the weighing of human character a more delicate sense of justice.

Chekhov is the dramatist of good-byes; good-byes to hopes and ambitions, good-byes between lovers. Yet out of this conception of life, which might be thought 'depressing', Chekhov makes a work of art which moves us and exalts us like a beautiful piece of music. It is not in a mood of depression one leaves the theatre after seeing *The Three Sisters*. How true it is that a good play should be like a piece of music! For our reason it must have the logical coherence of fact, but for our emotions the sinuous unanalysable appeal of music. In and out, in and out, the theme of hope for the race and the theme of personal despair are interwoven one with the other. Each character is like a different instrument which leads and gives way alternately, sometimes playing alone, sometimes with others, the theme of the miseries of cultivated exiles, or the deeper one of the longing of youth; the dreamy, once gay Irena, the sober and steady Olga, the passionate Masha, half ashamed of her greedy clutch on happiness—vulgarizing herself, she knows, but not caring for that. And what queer harsh notes proceed from that black pit of egotistic megalomania and ferocious diffidence, Solyony! Solyony thought himself a romantic Lermontov; nowadays he would pride himself on being a ruthless superman of the underworld. *Plus ca change, plus c'est la même chose.*

IVANOV

1925

"O what a rogue and peasant slave am I"

THE STAGE SOCIETY last week gave one of their very best performances. *Ivanov* is one of the least known of Chekhov's plays. It
is not counted among his best, and yet how good it is! It was
his first attempt at a big play, and it failed. Towards the end of
his life he re-wrote it and improved it immensely; it was played
by the Moscow Art Theatre, and again it did not succeed. The
reason of this second failure was (I have good authority for saying this) that the Moscow company did not bring out the comedy
of the piece. They played it too tearfully, just as the English
company the other day missed the rainbow effects, laughter
through tears, in *The Cherry Orchard*. In *Ivanov* the strain of
comedy is far stronger, and it was clearly brought out in Mr
Komisarjevsky's production.

Ivanov is generally described as Chekhov's attempt to write a
Russian *Hamlet*, and the description is a good one. Ivanov, the
principal figure, is a man whose will has been broken, and the
line I have quoted at the top of this article runs like a refrain
through all his speeches. He is sick with self-disgust. Before the
curtain rises we are given to understand that he was a particularly fine specimen among Russian landowners, an active, aspir-
ing, generous young man of high ability. He married for love a
Jewess whose rich parents discarded her for making a 'mixed
marriage'. You remember that in Hamlet's case, too, we must
understand that the young Prince was full of promise. We
catch through that play glimpses of the earlier Hamlet; in
Chekhov's play (I think this is a defect in it), there is only one
flash of the hero's quondam spirit. It tells in his last cry, 'My
youth has come back—the old Ivanov is alive again'—uttered
just before he shoots himself, but it occurs nowhere else.

During the rest of the play he is exhibited to us as helpless,
morbid, vacillating, crushed by shame. Now it is exceedingly

difficult to bring out the tragic quality of emotions which hearty, healthy people, let alone the medical profession, label as pathological. It is in this respect that actors usually fail in acting Hamlet and Romeo. (The hysterical Romeo, for instance, especially in the scene with the Friar, seldom touches us.) Mr Robert Farquharson's Ivanov succeeded wonderfully in conveying a vivid sense of inner tension and refinement. It is not easy to hold our sympathy in such a part as Ivanov, and yet it is all important that we should distinguish between Ivanov himself, who is a good man, and the view which all the characters save two, Sasha and her simple amiable old tippler of a father, take of his character. He brings misery into the lives of all near him; he fails to act consistently; his motives are open to misinterpretation by malicious gossips. His agent, Borkin, is responsible for this, but such gossip is also the result of Ivanov's reckless self-depreciation. In a notable passage of self-condemnation Ivanov compares himself to a vain young peasant who broke his back shouldering, out of swagger, a load far too heavy for him. What is the load Ivanov has to carry?

Firstly, disappointment, and provincial life—its pettiness and dullness have proved stronger than his enthusiasms. Secondly, bankruptcy: and last, but not least, he has ceased to love his wife, his sick, beautiful, lonely Anna (excellently played by Miss de Casalis), towards whom he has by no means ceased to feel nevertheless a tender loyalty. Against his will he has often found comfort in the companionship of Sasha, a young girl, the daughter of a rich, miserly mother. Her attraction for him is that of credulous, admiring, energetic youth for a tired, sceptical man who has lost faith in himself. To the neighbours it looks as though, disappointed in one rich marriage, he was preparing to make another; they know Anna is consumptive and cannot live long. She is on Ivanov's nerves; and both the doctor, who attends Anna and is in love with her himself, and Ivanov's neighbours think he is only too ready to hasten the poor woman's death by treating her badly. Ivanov's self-accusations seem to bear them out.

Sasha is a character to be met in the pages of Turgenev, but here she is not idealized. She is in love with Ivanov and it is she who does the wooing. Her passion is distinguishable from a longing to help him; she is the type of girl who loves a man because she believes she can 'save' him. But Ivanov does not believe he can be saved; he feels on the contrary that he will drag Sasha down. The death of poor Anna is heavy on his conscience in the last act. On his wedding morning, though he refuses to go to church, Sasha will not release him. Is she in love with him or with her own goodness? Both. There is a comi-tragic competition in unselfishness between them, amazing to her plain-minded father, Lebediev, and then—Ivanov shoots himself.

Those who have not seen the play will wonder where in such a story comedy could come in. Well, the answer is, it is by Chekhov. It is in these humiliations and self-regarding scruples of the hero that the comedy lies; in the contrast between him and such simple, kindly souls as Lebediev and such eupeptic thick-skinned vulgarians as Borkin (gloriously acted by Mr George Hayes); in the fact, so true to life, that gossip makes the most private perplexities of the soul also, alas, the concern of people who conspicuously leave that element out in judging people. This vague hum of lively indifference and callous censoriousness of which gossip is composed was wonderfully rendered in the production. The party at the Lebedievs' house was a masterpiece of stage craft. Indeed, the whole production was one which the playgoer can look back upon and say, 'I have seen Chekhov properly acted.'

ENGLISH PLAYS

JOHN GALSWORTHY

THE MOB

1914

UNTIL EVIDENCE is forthcoming, I am determined to think that *The Mob* (now being acted—and well acted—by Miss Horniman's company at the Coronet Theatre) is a very early play which has lain in Mr Galsworthy's drawer fifteen years. Its theme was a burning one when the Boer War was on. I like to think of him as a young man sitting down to write this play, championing the loyalty of those who dared cry ' stop the war'; and I regret that an MS, then so opportune, should have vainly gone the round of the managers during the Khaki campaign. And since this had to be, I like to suppose that it is now only a sense of the importance of the principles the play upholds which has induced Mr Galsworthy to allow an early work, otherwise unworthy of him to be performed. For, however belated, the play does deal with a theme which has permanent significance. It is the conflict between two kinds of patriotism, or more generally between 'the mob' and the lonely propagandist—the theme of *The Enemy of the People*, 'the majority is always wrong'); though in Ibsen's play the patriotism in question was local, not national. *The Mob* is therefore not out of date. Let anyone who is inclined to talk about slaying the slain and buried reflect what an arch body-snatcher and resurrectionist Father Time is. But it is particularly unfortunate in this case that the play should not have nicked its moment; for what might then have passed as a bold contribution to a bitter controversy must now be judged as a work of art, and it cannot stand that test.

Stephen Moor (Mr Milton Rosmer was, I felt, exactly what Mr Galsworthy meant his hero to be) is a young Minister of State at a time when England declares war upon a weak, semi-civilized nation. He sacrifices his career, his friends, the affection of his family, and ultimately his life, in protesting against a policy which he feels to be barbarous, greedy, and unjust. It is particularly difficult for him to take such a line publicly, because his wife comes of a military family; her father is in the War Office, her brothers are soldiers. Stephen Moor is, in fact, surrounded with the sort of people who understand his conduct least; to whom any man who weighs the rights and wrongs of his country's cause when Englishmen are actually suffering and dying for it at the front, let alone one who openly sympathises with the enemy's side of the quarrel, appears inevitably as a most unpleasant, incomprehensible compound of traitor and prig. Honestly, they can only account for such an attitude in a public man by supposing him possessed by an itch to make himself out better than his neighbours or a fellow who wants advertisement at any cost.

Now, there are two kinds of patriots; one who feels that 'my country right or wrong' is the only motto for a man with generous, warm, human feelings, and another who could not love his country so much loved he not her honour more. Stephen is such a patriot. He knows he cannot stop the war, but he is determined that 'history shall not say when England did this thing not a voice was raised in protest'. He feels, too, though his efforts will be vain, that they are the birth-throes of a finer kind of national consciousness. Why, he asks, should not a country behave to another with the chivalry and fairness everybody admits the strong should show to the weak? And if love of one's country is so high a virtue, why crush it in a little nation? He judges his country's conduct by the standards we apply to individuals.

It must be confessed that so tested all nations come out badly. I am sure if you or I met Britannia and Germania in the flesh, we should dislike them very much. What a couple of vulgar, greedy, touchy old women they would be! Can't you imagine them talking incessantly about their pedigrees, swaggering about their acres and incomes, and flying, if they thought they had been done out of half-a-crown, into a vindictive fluster and swearing they would be in the workhouse next? Vilely inconsiderate both of them to people in their power; bridling like turkey-cocks, with panic in one eye and menace in the other when they came up against anyone formidable? The behaviour of nations is certainly inferior to that of the better sort of people in them. They are generally to be admired only for their strength. This is precisely the quality which excites the patriotism of 'the mob'.

Mr Galsworthy has set out to draw an heroic figure in conflict with this kind of patriotism. A hero is always difficult to draw; it is so easy, and so fatal, to be sentimental about him. Among my readers there must be many who indulge in daydreams, and some of them will know the kind of day-dream which is woven round the idea of how lovely it would be to be martyred. To stand up in the eye of the world, protesting to the last, vehement, firm, too lofty to retaliate, a victim of blind stupidity that knows too late what it has done—such a dream is a pleasant variant to visions of prodigious personal triumphs. Bad fiction, bad plays,—one recognises the source of their inspiration; they are such stuff as day-dreams are made of.

Mr Galsworthy's Stephen Moor is a rather more objective study, but there hangs about the play a flavour of the day-dream. The dramatist has placed him in circumstances which should make his ordeal particularly cruel; he had to sacrifice the affection and respect of those he cares for most. Well and good. But Mr Galsworthy has not made the painfulness of these scenes rasping enough. The quarrel over the dinner table on which the curtain rises is not excruciating; the scenes afterwards between Stephen and his wife when she tries to restrain him from starting on his anti-war campaign are flat; Stephen is gentle, dignified, and depressed; she is reproachful and depressed—consequently, *we* are depressed. These characters are not endowed with that urgent temperamental directness which brings truth out dramatically. Each antagonist only represents languidly a point of view.

All through Stephen remains, in a weak sense, a dignified, pathetic figure. His election committee throws him over (Act II); he is pelted with orange peel and stones (Act III); his servants give notice, his wife leaves him (Act IV, Scene I). And when a British victory occurs a mafficking mob enters his house for a spree (Act IV), carries him round on its shoulders singing 'What's the matter with Stephie', and then, when he abuses it, kills him. (This assault was not well stage-managed.) The frightened revellers melt away; but one remains to lay a paper Union Jack upon the breast of the dead, genuine patriot. Then the curtain rises for the last time to enable us to read a laudatory inscription upon a bronze statue of the young statesman. The fickleness of public opinion is proved.

Here you will say are sufferings enough to enable us to estimate the mettle of a hero. No. In effect they are merely circumstances flattering to a vanity which imagines itself in his place. Stephen's sufferings are like the halo which in an old-fashioned print of a drowned Christian martyr hovers above the dark waters where she floats, 'young and so fair'. Everything that happens to him is most becoming. His wife leaves him with the words 'You are too noble for me' on her lips, while he exhibits a sympathetic modesty. 'Do you suppose I compare myself with the meanest private out there ?' he says (a false note in a man who is sustained by the conviction that he is fighting to bring a finer patriotism into the world). He is struck by a stone, which stamps his forehead with the red seal of courage— not by rotten eggs. The fault of the play is that Moor's sufferings are distinctly decorative; and Mr Galsworthy has not spared the accessories which add external touches of pathos: Stephen's little daughter (always in her 'nighty') runs babbling in and out (and very prettily Miss Phyllis Bourke did it); strains of street music are timely; a wine-glass snaps in Stephen's steady hand (Act I). But the *inward* stress of his struggle and the pathos of that was not 'done' at all.

Heroes are often pathetic. A fine man losing his fineness in a raucous nerve-wracking wrangle, sacrificing not only his peace but his virtues and dignity to a cause—that is the spectacle which can make us thrill and weep. Orange peel and an occasional stone are trifles. It is in deeper humiliations, in finding himself unable to meet at all points the other side, and compelled to bluff and juggle however right in the main; in discovering that he appeals to those he does not respect as much as he does his enemies—it is in such experiences the bitterness of standing alone lies. If in Act II, instead of being discarded by his local caucus, an incident which might have been taken for granted, we had seen cranks and ninnies flocking round Stephen Moor as his father-in-law prophesied they would; if in Act III he had returned home fagged out for one night's rest and had to parry the interminable nagging of a bitter, faithful woman, we should have got a better notion of what he was going through.

It is a common device of dramatists to suggest the climax of a hero's sacrifice by making his wife leave him. But our sense of the tragedy depends upon the idea they have previously succeeded in giving us of the wife in question; and they often forget this. Katherine Moor could not live with her husband after her brother had been killed in the war. But we only saw husband and wife when they were out of sympathy. What she was to him at other times had to be taken for granted; as far as we could see she was not a woman from whom it would be very painful to part.

In Act III Mr Galsworthy succumbed to the bedroom scene. Only in this case it was staged with great austerity—the bedroom had no bed in it. The point of the stage bedroom is, in comedy, the curious pleasure of gazing upon a bed; in scenes of high emotion, that the heroine may without incongruity let down her back hair like the old tragedy queens. There were Mrs Moor and her sister-in-law, their hair ringing out like wild bells to the night; the latter seeing a vision of her husband dying beside a gun on the field of battle, and the former offering connubial caresses, as bribes, to a husband presumably hoarse and battered from the hustings. In Stephen Moor's ruthful departure from the room, leaving his wife fallen forward in shame upon the absent bed, there was that which reminded me of King Arthur's withdrawal from Guinevere. The best scene in the play was that in which Stephen's father-in-law tells him that England has won a victory, and then, that Katherine's brother has been killed. Mr. Lomas acted the old general well.

GRANVILLE BARKER

THE MADRAS HOUSE

1925

WHEN I CALLED once on Mr George Moore, after not having seen him for over a year, in the course of conversation he broke out enthusiastically, 'I have never forgotten a thing you once said to me'. Radiant with appreciation, he proceeded to repeat what I remembered distinctly he had once said to *me*. This incident made an impression. So, when I read the other day a paragraph about myself in which I was praised as a talker, I felt that if the writer had only said, 'He is one of the best listeners of the day', though, in the context, such a compliment might have appeared ironical, I could have said, 'I understand what you mean and I thank you', and concluded that the writer was a careful reader of my dramatic criticisms. It is an elementary quality for a critic to plume himself upon, but, when I go to the theatre, I do *listen*.

It is a quality which is particularly necessary in the case of *The Madras House*. To appreciate *The Madras House* you must be 'a listener'; you must listen not only to the ideas which are discussed from time to time, not only to the commonplaces and snappishnesses of the dialogue, but to the constant inaudible implications of temperament and habit. Then, I promise you rare pleasures.

You need not think during the performance. It is a mistake to think during a play. People suppose that the so-called "highbrow' plays require you to think, and very reasonably they say, 'We don't go to the theatre to think'. No, don't think *in* the theatre, but listen; let the play soak in—think afterwards. There are plays which only require you to look; there are others which only require you to feel. and there are also plays which ask you to listen. Chekhov's plays make this demand and, therefore, one might expect that recent appreciation of Chekhov would have prepared the way for the appreciation of Mr Granville Barker's plays, and that people had acquired the habit of listening in the theatre. Yet I doubt this result of recent enthusiasm for Chekhov. Chekhov is a very emotional dramatist; Mr Granville Barker's drama is emotionally distinctly dry. It is a most interesting dryness, but his greatest defect as a playwright is an excess of emotional asceticism. This was particularly noticeable in the love passages in *The Voysey Inheritance*, where the girl, against the author's intention, turns into a prig.

Here, too, when the situation between his characters reaches the most serious pitch, instead of speaking impulsively out of themselves, they tend to transfer their predicament to the plane of generalities, discussing it as one not peculiar to themselves but to many. (*Vide* the dialogue between husband and wife with which *The Madras House* closes.) In short the drama of Granville Barker is that of a man to whom the significance of life has been most excitingly revealed, not at moments when, so to speak, he has banged up against other human beings, but when intimacy has taken the form of sounding the depths of experience together, and the condition of mutual proximity has been on both sides a high personal detachment. I can imagine Mr Granville Barker when taxed with introducing too much 'talk' into his plays, in proportion to 'drama', opening his eyes with some surprise and asking in return if the critic cannot remember 'talks' which in their effect upon his life, in bringing this or that tendency to a climax in himself, had not been as dramatic as any 'event'.

The youngest of the principal masculine characters in *The Madras House*, Philip Madras, is a man of this temperament in an accentuated form, and as might be guessed the Man-Woman Problem is one which naturally presents itself to such a one in a peculiarly intimate manner. Difference of sex at once makes ʾor intimacy and disturbs the detachment, that impersonal detachment in intimacy, which for Philip Madras is the intensest form of living. The Man-Woman Problem has been the subject

of countless plays in which the psychology of relations between
the sexes has been the theme, but I think it may be claimed for
The Madras House that the peculiar aspect of it (an important
one), which Philip Madras is the means of throwing into relief,
has never been so curiously and delicately treated on the stage.
The rest of the play is about other aspects of the same theme,
seen from the point of view of men and women of different
temperaments and differently circumstanced, all of which have
been treated in drama and fiction many times.

Mr. Granville Barker's method is to unite superficially
(chiefly connected through business or family relations) a
number of men and women, and make them talk. What they
talk about are the incidents of a couple of days not more closely
interconnected than incidents usually are; the return of a father
from the East who thirty years ago deserted his family and
turned Mohammedan, adopting the Eastern solution of sex
questions; the fact that a girl in a huge dressmakers' establishment is going to have a baby (an employer's problem), and that
the huge business is bought by an American man of business.

If you listen carefully to the dialogue of *The Madras House*
you will get the essence of several dramas. It is equivalent to
reading, say, *Au Bonheur des Dames*, a play about spinsters
withering on the stalk, a play about the defiant young 'woman
who did', and a play, say, by M Porto Riche, about the hash
made of a man's work by woman's attractiveness. And here we
touch the explanation of the form. Only in the conversation
drama can so many aspects of a theme (here the Man-Woman
relation) be treated. It is the quickest form; when Mr Shaw
wanted to present at once all the sides of the marriage problem
he, in *Getting Married*, was forced to adopt it. To bring out a
huge theme in action takes much longer.

There was no alternative open to Mr Granville Barker besides
writing a conversation play and writing six action plays on sex.
Do you ask why he did not write then the six plays ? Well there
is an advantage in presenting the essence of each aspect inter-
locked and together. We can get a bird's eye view of a gigantic

theme much too big for treatment in a single action drama. He
has constructed his conversation drama with a skill which it is a
delight to remember afterwards. I can understand a spectator
thinking that the dramatist was spending too much time on the
construction of a realistic atmosphere, but on reflection these
little touches, like the perpetual polite introductions of the
many daughters of Mr Huxtable (Admirable, perfect Mr Aubrey
Mather!) to Major Thomas, are superfluous. Not at all. They
suggest the dire extent to which human relationships in that
household have been fossilised into prim formalities, just as the
mannequin show illustrates the 'moral' and commercial exploi-
tation of sex interest.

Mr Shaw in his conversation dramas does not care a hang
about surface plausibility; in Mr Granville Barker's drama the
naturalness of every word spoken and every detail is as important to his effects as it is in Chekov's. Under his own direction
this perfect naturalness of delivery and gesture was achieved by
every actor and actress on the stage. I want particularly to mention the acting of Miss Irene Rooke in the dismal, whining part
of Amelia Madras, because it is such an ungrateful one. Everybody cheers when the vivacious Mr Windlesham or the pre-
posterous, commercial, sentimental American leaves the stage,
and excellently Mr Ernest Milton and Mr Claud Rains played
them; but the chill damp discomfort which Mrs Madras so
properly spreads round her on the stage does not promote
vociferous applause. Yet how important it was that she should
be duly dank! Everybody sees at once how good Miss Agnes
Thomas was as the strict and desiccated spinster, but the perfection of the sketch of the middle-class *grande dame*, for once
not ridiculed (Bravo! Mr Granville Barker and Miss Frances
Ivor) might possibly escape notice.

The character-drawing and its interpretation is throughout a
joy to an amateur of human nature. It is full of subtle touches
that delight me, such as the hint which the old Pasha papa
Madras incautiously gives to his daughter-in-law that he is the
father of the shop-girl's baby; so, too, Philip's comment on

hearing of it; 'If he hadn't been, he'd love us to believe it! Vanity! His real spur, I do verily believe, to that fine and flamboyantly amorous career'—which also throws light on Philip, who could never, however hard he tried, completely understand his father's attitude towards women; so, too, Philip's comment on his friend Hippisly Thomas's reserve about his wife: Thomas is no Mohammedan in practice, is Thomas, but he can understand the old Pasha very well. 'No nice husband discusses his wife', says Philip of him; 'Upon sound Mohammedan principles, he guards her in the harem of his heart'. It is the spiritual purdah that Philip wants to tear down.

Thus the play is a scheme of ingeniously contrived talk through which illuminating rays from different temperamental quarters are thrown on the theme. Old Madras is a man to whom sex is the spice of life, but he does not like the whole of life to be flavoured with it; the sentimental American, Mr Eustace Perrin State, wants every dish saturated with it—but in a diluted, romantic form; old Huxtable has thought all his life that the proper thing to do was to ignore it—and a nice mess the Huxtable family have made of that. The point of view of the desiccated Miss Chancellor is given, and—wonder of wonders —she is properly allowed to keep her dignity, in the hands of a lesser draughtsman she would have been just a poor old cock-shy; the young mother who has thrown her cap over the wind-mill gives hers; the cramped and harried Brigstocks exhibit the predicament into which industrial civilisation has forced them; and Philip Madras—I have indicated his position.

The weakness of the play lies in the last conversation between Philip and his wife, where also not a few of the finest touches are found. The impression this leaves behind is too indistinct. The bit about Philip's experiences as a lecturer is not wanted; it is one of the few passages in the play which is really otiose. We don't want to know more than that Philip is a man who wants to help to put the world straight, and that has been indi-cated. Mr Granville Barker has, I believe, rewritten this scene, but he has not yet got it right. In the finest human relation

possible, man and woman must be alike—that is *his* philosophy.
Perhaps. The play at any rate suggests, through Jessica Madras,
that it is pretty nearly impossible. The curtain would emphasise
this point if it fell on her words 'But you can't be wise for us'—
better, I think, would be the words 'Don't, whatever you do, be
too wise'.

You must listen to this play to get anything out of it; if you
are going to wonder what became of Marion Yates and her baby,
instead of keeping your attention on the theme, you had better
not go.

SOMERSET MAUGHAM

OUR BETTERS

1923

I DO NOT KNOW if Mr Somerset Maugham, who has travelled a great deal lately, has visited M Coué at Nancy, but certainly every day and in every way his work gets better and better. This is as it should be with successful dramatists, yet how far more usual it is to begin well and tail off! Mr Maugham, after a period of vain endeavour, I understand about as long as the briefless period of an able but unconnected young barrister, suddenly blazed into success. The first time I heard of him, though he had already written a grim, pathetic and remarkable little novel, he was being interviewed by the papers as an astoundingly fortunate young man who had actually three plays running in London at the same time. This was certainly an unusual triumph, but one not which excited my curiosity; indeed, looking back, I see I was then so convinced that a certain measure of ill-success was the concomitant of merit, that this put me off. Thenceforth, like everybody else, when a Maugham play appeared with expected frequency, I took a long run for granted; but, as a critic, that the play would not furnish me matter for discourse.

I went to one or two. They were eminently actable; they had the handy compactness, the shop-finish and alluring shininess of a new dressing-case. The dialogue was clear, but the diction like Pinero's, was insensitive. I was not interested till *Home and Beauty* opened my eyes to the fact that Mr Maugham had, in addition to his solid stage aptitudes, a far prettier gift for comedy than I had supposed. And I discovered something else; that his gift sprang from a clear-sighted, hard-edged cynicism, rare in English writers; it was Latin, in quality. It came later to the surface, here and there, in *The Unknown*; it disappeared again in a play so negligible that I am no longer sure of its name—Miss Marie Lohr was the heroine and there was a kind-hearted doctor in it; and, to my joy, it fairly dominated his next play, *The Circle*. There the flavour of it was a little too pungent for palates which had relished *Lady Frederick*, etc. Yet in America, oddly enough, *The Circle* was a prodigious success. They must have been too innocent to feel its devastating implications; for as a rule no people strike one as more determined than Americans to insist that life is a crescendo of happiness or more prone to regard cynicism as treason. *East of Suez*, which followed, was an obvious compromise with the raree-show traditions of His Majesty's: I took it as such. The masculine characters in it were conventional and negligible; but the woman in it was admirably portrayed. She was a creation of that attention, at once indulgent and hard, characteristic of Mr Maugham, which when directed upon certain feminine types, enables him to present them alive upon the stage, with their energies, duplicities, passions and trivialities.

Consequently, having taken *East of Suez* as a work constructed to meet rather unfortunate theatrical conditions, I went to the Globe Theatre with *The Circle* still uppermost in my mind.

Having arrived, then, at a general notion of the kind of play Mr Maugham was born to write, the critical question for me was whether or not he was going to proceed along lines which, with the arrogance which is one of the drawbacks of the critical temperament, I had peremptorily decided he ought to travel: and I was delighted. With the exception of a single kink—one episode in which the dramatist had seemed to wince and refrain —the play went deep and straight, directed from beginning to end by what I believe to be Mr Maugham's true instinct as an artist.

The people who are presented as 'Our Betters' are Lady George Grayson, the Duchesse de Surennes, the Principessa della Cercola, the rich, bumptiously and sentimentally possessive Arthur Fenwick, the impecunious Tony Paxton and Thornton Clay, 'who calls more countesses by their Christian names than any other man in London'. The curtain has not been up many minutes before we grasp the irony of the title.

The play itself is a mercilessly amusing picture of a rootless, fruitless, extremely vulgar, smart set of people; a much paragraphed, photographed set, whose habits are luxurious, whose standards are common and cynical, whose love-affairs, relieved by a certain engaging candour, are canine. And who are the ladies with high-sounding names? They are American heiresses who have married for rank.

As far as experience enables me to check the verisimilitude of the general picture, the dramatist has stressed their nationality unfairly. All the characters in the set, sympathetic as well as vulgar, are American, with the exception of the fair Tony, who gets his living in it by complaisances which used to be considered unmasculine and dishonourable, and of the harmless Lord Bleane, who fails to secure in the end his scared young transatlantic heiress. This stressing of nationality has, however, two advantages from the point of view of success: in England the play in its implications will have the air of being confined to a merely alien portion of the fashionable rich—though, goodness knows, our social soil produces 'Pearl's' and 'Minnie's'; while in America its satire will seem directed only against a small, and naturally unpopular group of denationalised American snobs.

Yet satire is not the right word to describe the play. It is only a 'satire' for those who attribute to the author their own moral reactions to what he shows them. Each character is allowed rope, and if, at the end of the performance, in your estimation the whole set is left dangling from the gibbet, either it was *you* who strung them up or they hanged themselves; it was not Mr Maugham who put on the black cap. *Our Betters* is rather a sardonically detached comedy; an exposure in the manner of Maupassant of one luxuriant corner of the social jungle. If it had entered Miss Margaret Bannerman's head (she gave us an extraordinarily good performance) that Pearl Grayson was a satire on the smart modern hostess, the play would have been lost. Happily she had imagination enough to play Pearl with delicious appreciation, and intelligence enough to expect us also to delight, like naturalists, in the admirable equipment of some sly, swift animal; in Pearl's witty agility, her shameless courage, her claws and caresses, her gorgeous silly snobbishness, her tight, ferocious clutch upon money and prestige. Against a background of spiritual values, or the heart, Pearl shows up as indeed graceless and ignoble; but against the background of her own world she has a certain lustre; not so the duchess Minnie, whose comical, helpless lack of dignity, whining amorousness, and sluggish, hysterical malevolence Miss Collier acted profoundly well. Pearl is a very vulgar woman, but still she has 'form'—however bad—and gay effrontery; Minnie is a shapeless jelly-fish that stings when trodden upon.

When to expose it Maupassant explored the *demi-monde* in *Yvette*, he used the panic of a girl who believed her surroundings to be dazzling and enviable. Elizabeth Saunders, Pearl's sister fresh from America and an heiress herself, also at first believes her sister's *monde* to be splendid. The invisibility of Lord George, and the ill-mannered ubiquity of Arthur (excellently played by Mr Drayton), who pays Pearl's bills; the cynical conversation of the set, their insensitive discussion of her private affairs (it is taken for granted she has hooked Lord Bleane) surprise but do not deeply disturb her. When the play opens she is thoroughly used to the atmosphere, and ready to believe she cannot do better than imitate her sister Pearl. The arrival, however, of a young American lover who is a fish out of water, increases her hesitation to take the worldly matrimonial plunge. She puts off Lord Bleane. She will give him an answer when they meet again at Pearl's country house. It is there (Arthur, as usual, is a quasi-host) she gets her scare.

We have already seen Pearl handling him and heard, too, how she talks of him behind his back; her methods are the admiration of her friends. Tony, who finds dependence on the too exactingly amorous Minnie very trying, has a fancy for

Pearl, who is herself as dependent on Arthur. There is a rapid scene between them: 'Let's go down to the tea-house.' 'No I won't.' 'We shall be quite safe there.' 'I daren't, it's too risky.' 'Oh, damn the risk.' Pearl arranges poker for the rest of the party and they disappear. But the lynx-eyed Minnie has seen them go. While the cards are being dealt she exclaims that she has left her bag with her money in the garden tea-house; Lord Bleane gets up to get it. He returns saying he can't find it, and Elizabeth volunteers to hunt, for it must be there; on which Lord Bleane becomes agitated. 'No, no, don't go—besides the door is locked.' 'Oh, it can't be,' says the Duchesse, quietly, 'I saw Pearl and Tony go in just now.' Elizabeth bursts into tears; the Princess jumps up, 'Minnie, you devil!' . . . The game goes on; Fenwick with distorted face dealing and muttering, 'The slut, the slut!' Elizabeth sobbing, presently the absent couple stroll airily in. Here was the test of the dramatist! The quick closing dialogue is a triumph. Pearl has barely begun her bland excuse before she grasps what has happened. She turns to Tony: 'You damned fool, I told you it was too risky.' The fall of the curtain hides what we gather, in the next act, to have been a very ugly row; the Duchesse in hysterics and Arthur in little better, though he would no doubt have described it as a strong man's wrath. And it is in this last act that Mr Maugham, I think, shows his remarkable power. The sardonic comedy of anti-climax is here of the first order. The kink in his treatment of his subject, which I mentioned above, is, of course, that it should have been *Elizabeth* who went for the bag, and *her* agitation which produced the disclosure; for it is her distress, her *volte face* which is the pivot of the play.

Doubtless Mr Maugham thought this, however, too excruciating a turn to give the scene, and the explosion is still most effective. It leaves Pearl with two objects; to get back Arthur and to prevent her party breaking up and her friends spreading the story. Her successful contrivances are as remorselessly comic as Minnie's reconciliation with Tony, to whom she offers marriage. The emotional squalor of these people's relations, the absence of anything approaching loyalty between them, is coolly exposed. Their lack of all standards, even of superficial elegance, is deliciously suggested by their enthusiastic reception of Ernest, on whose egregious vulgarity and capers the curtain descends.

I have not mentioned the Princess (Miss Marion Terry is beautifully natural in the part); she is of, but not happy in, this group of *Our Betters*, and she is the mouthpiece of the explanation: how it was that the lure of romance has decoyed these women into trashy snobbery. Her character is another test of her environment. *

SHEPPEY

1933

YES IT IS a comedy, but a comedy which borders upon drama, and even upon religious drama. It begins in the saloon of a fashionable hairdresser's shop in Jermyn Street, and it ends with a dialogue between a hairdresser's assistant and Death. In Act I and II comedy predominates, but the drama lies in contrast between the spirit of Christian charity and what passes for the Christian religion in the world. Some of the humour is grim. You could not have a much bitterer joke than a young daughter clasping her pretty little hands in an agony of supplication and imploring 'Oh God make father potty'. But most of the humour lies in lines revealing selfish snobbishness and

* In the following issue of *The New Statesman* Mr Maugham wrote to say that it was the Censor who had objected to Elizabeth being the one to discover the lovers in the garden tea-house, and that he had altered the play to meet that objection: a very good example of the sort of public interference to which dramatists are subjected in this country.

genteel aspirations, and spoken by those who do not realise what they have betrayed. Here Mr Maugham has always excelled.

In earlier days I would have expected that Mr Somerset Maugham in treating such a theme would have written more out of his contempt for what he disliked than out of his sympathy for whatever contrasted with it. Contempt for human nature, and an indulgence towards it equally scornful, has hitherto been his strongest suit whenever he has deviated from comedy proper. The reason why that admirable play *For Services Rendered* did not hold the public for long (many enjoyed it and admired it—under protest), was that positive sympathy, as contrasted with satirical exposure, found in it no counter-balancing expression. For the discerning and tough-minded this did not detract from their response to the play, but there was no character in it on which the popular imagination could rest with complete satisfaction.

Here, in this play, it is not so. The character in it which is most vividly conceived is Sheppey the barber, who is compact of natural kindliness and goodness. No qualities are more moving on the stage than these, but they are exceedingly difficult to handle without tipping over into sentiment. The dramatist must avoid showing that he is touched by them himself. Mr Maugham has not sentimentalised Sheppey, even when his inexhaustible and spontaneous 'charity' approaches the gospel ideal. Sheppey is not a saviour of souls; he cannot save the petty thief or the public-house tart. He is not interested in them because they have immortal souls, let alone as citizens, but because he cannot help liking them as they are, even when he wishes they were different. He is shocked by misery and unhappiness but be cannot be disgusted by human beings, whatever they do. As one of the characters remarks, Sheppey has no moral sense whatever. Galsworthy once drew such a character—Wellwyn in *The Pigeon*, which, to my mind, was one of his best pieces of work.

How does Mr Maugham modulate from a fashionable hairdresser's shop to the theme of Christian charity? It is deftly done, and there are two points about the management of the transition which will excite the admiration of those who know anything about the playwright's craft.

First, the character of Sheppey, revealed to us while he is shaving customers and chatting with the other assistants, is (though at the time no such interest enters our heads) exactly the right soil out of which the flower of Christian charity might plausibly spring, granted some sudden opening, illumination or religious conversion—or whatever you like to call it—takes place. What made Sheppey the perfect barber, and the soul of the establishment he served, was his *humility*; that old-fashioned but important virtue, and the one, oddly enough, which often makes a man trust his intuitions against the judgment of the world. Without drawing our attention to it directly, the playwright has suggested Sheppey's natural humility, by exhibiting his wholehearted devotion to his little job; and it was his quality which Mr Richardson's masterly impersonation of every side of Sheppey's character, brought out so well. Not long ago we saw Mr Richardson in *Wild Decembers* as the curate who wooed Charlotte Brontë—successfully at last. Once again he shows a rare understanding of human goodness, and a rare restraint in expressing it; Mr Richardson is again a perfect interpreter of a dramatist's subtler intentions, and in a part, too, which requires a nice adjustment between humour and deep feeling.

The second point about Mr Maugham's transition is the ingenious use of what may be described as 'the red herring'.

Two very important things happened to Sheppey that morning in Jermyn Street. He had had to attend the police court as the principal witness in the case of a man who stole an overcoat from a car; and while listening to his own and other cases he had been strangely upset. The criminals and outcasts of society are human beings like himself and as amiable as his customers! Hunger and misery had made them what they were; Sheppey is so disturbed by this discovery that he cannot help chatting about his amazement.

The second, is the news that he has won £8,500 in the Irish

Sweepstake. When the curtain falls on the establishment drinking Sheppey's health in champagne, we are naturally left guessing how his luck is going to affect him. I must mention that he has brought in with him a woman from the public house opposite, with whom he had often had a little friendly talk, discovering, now, she is hungry and exhausted; and that when he and she are left alone together, he has a slight fit—probably the result of suppressed excitement. Well, how is his sweepstake luck going to affect him and the story ? I do not suppose a single person in the theatre anticipated the actual consequences. I know several alternatives, each in Mr Maugham's vein, occurred to me, and not one of them proved right; he might be paralysed by another stroke and his 'luck' turn out a curse, or his wife, whom we had not seen, might be a tiresome silly woman who would destroy the contented life he had hitherto led by her pursuit of silly social ambitions, or she might be furiously jealous of the woman who brought him home that night; or again, the money might spoil Sheppey himself—in his middle-age he might turn vulgar-gay and rush to ruin.

But Act II shows Mrs Sheppey to be charming, sensible, steady; and, gradually, it is disclosed that Sheppey's experience in the police court, together with his fit (probably this was accompanied by some strange spiritual illumination as with Dostoievsky), have together implanted in him a very different longing. He has forgotten his day-dreams of buying a nice little house and providing a slap-up wedding for his daughter, who is engaged to a pushful young schoolmaster in a county council school; he is resolved instead to give his money to all and sundry who clearly need it more than he does.

The conflict is not between husband and wife, but between Sheppey and the young couple, who see whisked away before their eyes the blessed chance of attaining the gentility they covet. Their dismay, their despair, are without bounds. No honeymoon trip to Paris for them; no marriage even perhaps for Sheppey's daughter (excellently played by Miss Angela Baddeley)—for she understands her Ernest, who conceals beneath the tags of a pretentious education and devotion to public service, the passions of a little arriviste. Ernest's arguments, and her violent clutch upon the money, make excellent comedy in contrast to Sheppey's buoyant insistence that the outcasts, the thief and the prostitute should come and live with them, and his determination (he only knows that this makes him happy) to scatter his fortune.

Such a sudden conversion to the ethics of the New Testament must be madness! He has failed to redeem the thief—who steals from him, or the prostitute—who runs off to the streets again, but these things matter not to Sheppey. He has obeyed his inmost impulse. If only the doctors would certify him! Mrs Sheppey also is deeply perturbed, especially when her husband turns down an offer of a partnership in the hair-dressing business, which in old days he had coveted before all things. Her husband is certainly in a queer state. But when the doctors diagnose his case as one of religious paranoia she is dismayed. (Here Mr Maugham indulges in some overcharged but effective satire of mental specialists.) Again we are left in doubt as to what will happen in the last act: a Strindberg ending of a loving woman fixing a straight-waistcoat on 'the father' seems a possibility. But Sheppey is lucky to the last. He is saved by death, and we from a painfully sardonic ending. He dies in a nap while his wife is out buying kippers for supper. There is a black-out, and the process of death is presented as a vision interrupted at one point by the reappearance of the thief. This dialogue is moving, but if death could have been a mere voice the effect would have been strengthened, and the confusion of one live figure and one subjective one being on the stage together, avoided.

Samuel Butler, looking back on the Christians who had surrounded him in his childhood, said that they would have been equally shocked by Christianity being denied, or taken seriously. This state of mind is the theme of the play, and it is deftly and firmly handled, and admirably interpreted, too, from the minor characters up to Sheppey himself.

THE CIRCLE

1944

THE CIRCLE has taken its place along with *Hamlet* and *Love for Love* in the first season of the Haymarket Theatre Repertory which will close on November 25. It is, as older playgoers will remember, a cynical comedy and the first of Somerset Maugham's really good plays. They will also recall that when first staged, in March, 1921, Lottie Venne played to perfection the part of 'Naughty' Lady Kitty, that once radiant reckless Victorian beauty, and Mr Thesiger the part of her fussy self-centred son, Arnold Champion Cheney, M.P.; with his nervous insistence on order and convention everywhere (natural enough after a boyhood made wretched by the scandalous notoriety of his mother) and his congruous love of eighteenth century 'interiors'. That remarkable first performance of the play had only one defect, which this reproduction remedies. Miss Fay Compton as Elizabeth Champion Cheney (Arnold's young wife) failed to present her as restless, and intense. I take up this old lapse in the career of an actress who went on to give us many admirable exhibitions of her art and who is now at her zenith, because it enables me to hail the young actress, Rosalie Crutchley, who now plays Elizabeth. I watched her carefully; I feel sure that she has a distinguished future. To-day, Mr Gielgud is the prim, nervous husband and Miss Yvonne Arnaud the over-blown ridiculous Lady Kitty, fighting a lost rear-guard action against time. Her delightful French accent is, of course, quite out of character, but she puts so much spirit into the part, such a gay recognition of what is ludicrous and pathetic in it that the audience is enraptured with Kitty's absurdities and tears. If she tends to act a little too much for *them* and not for the scene as a whole—well, that only disappoints a connoisseur in the art of the stage, and of such there are only a few in any audience. Mr Gielgud made an admirable tense prig with a grievance.

I

I do not understand why my colleague Mr Agate denies his gift for comedy: his Joseph Surface was far the best I ever saw.

Let me remind you of the play itself; it is, as I said, a cynical comedy, the first play by Somerset Maugham in which he exhibited uncompromisingly that estimate of human nature in general to which his best fiction had already owed its force. Cynicism is, of course, a vague term. What I mean by it is scepticism in regard to the depth and persistence of human affection, a conviction that men and women are competitive, ostentacious and selfish, and only superficially and erratically capable of disinterested sympathy; that time in the end gets the better of even the most intelligently self-seeking, though some consolation, *pro tem*, can be found in the amusements of luxury and the security of wealth. It is a point of view which bleakly stated is rejected by many who nevertheless act upon it. It has inspired more French than English writers. It is not, however, by any means intolerable to some who believe that to take a good look at the baseness of human nature is the best means towards honouring what is lovable in it.

Thus the cynic himself may not be as cynical as those he shocks. This, I think, is true of both Maupassant and Maugham.

When the curtain goes up on the drawing-room of the Champion Cheney's eighteenth-century country house (the décor is admirable) this young couple are faced with an extremely delicate situation. Elizabeth, after a good deal of domestic pressure, has at last succeeded in persuading her husband to allow her to invite her mother-in-law with Lord Porteous, who ran off with her thirty years ago. Arnold has not seen his mother since. Elizabeth has conceived a romantic idea of Lady Kitty, of her beauty and courage. She is bored and restless in her own marriage, and has a mind to a manly young tea-planter. One who dared all for love must be, she thinks, a wonderful woman. Unfortunately, Arnold's father arrives from Paris quite unexpectedly, while the old guilty couple, who have lived socially ostracised abroad, are motoring down. Elizabeth explains the situation to Arnold's father, who takes it calmly and seems inclined to withdraw. But he changes his mind when he gets a glimpse into his daughter-in-law's mind. The comedy which follows is admirable and a terrible disillusionment for Elizabeth. Instead of a sad, lovely, dignified heroine, Lady Kitty is a merry, silly, spasm-minded old creature, while her lover who sacrified a glorious political career for her, is a testy, nagging old man. Their flaring love-affair has guttered down into a sordid sort of marriage, and Mr Champion Cheney (excellently played by Mr Trouncer) takes every opportunity of stimulating squabbles between them, as an object lesson, a warning, to his romantically inclined daughter-in-law. She is depressed, especially by Lady Kitty's confession that though at first her elopement had been glorious, on the whole it had been a great mistake. But in spite of that, and in spite of advice which Mr Champion Cheney gave to his son (and he to the last thinks has done the trick), she bolts with her young colonial. The old lovers are moved to tears and laughter by an incident which recalls their own first careless raptures, though they know the young ones are fools. The play ends with the three old people laughing on the same sofa, for Champion Cheney has joined them to explain how he had succeeded in detaching Elizabeth from her lover. Is it a happy ending? Has the world been well lost for love this time? Or was the downy old Champion Cheney right? There is in the play no answer to these questions. It is not a full stop. but a recurring decimal dot. Life repeats itself; experience does not make for wisdom; men and women revolve 'in a circle'. It is a good play, full of laughter, some pity—for lost charms at any rate—and acute observation.

EAST OF SUEZ

1922

HIS MAJESTY'S is the home of pageant-drama; for any other purpose its huge stage is not only useless but a drawback. On those wide boards an actor must needs take exercise to convey even a slight impression of restlessness; from those distant galleries human faces are scarcely more expressive than the oval keys beneath a group picture. Subtleties of acting, and therefore subtleties of situation, are physically impossible upon it, and, moreover, a vast crowded auditorium is psychologically a sounding board only for certain dramatic effects. The dramatist writing for such a theatre should allow for this, and the critic must take account that he has had to do so. His Majesty's is the stage for the display of plain, popular emotions; the situations presented to so large an audience should be striking and easy. The majestic dramatist should borrow his technique from the opera and melodrama. He may, if he can, put even as much drawing into his characters as Shakespeare did, but like Shakespeare's, his situations must stand out comprehensible and arresting, even if ancillary touches are wasted and escape notice. I was impressed by the grasp Mr Somerset Maugham's *East of Suez* exhibited of these conditions. In the prologue he uses the capacity of the stage to present realistically a picture of swarming streets of Pekin, a scene not without bearing on his theme; in the last moment of the last act, when his half-cast heroine, whose father was an English merchant, is absorbed again into her maternal China, he has unblushingly and properly had recourse to a symbolic tableau. There Miss Meggie Albanesi sits as the curtain falls, hieratic and impassable in Chinese robes, with her beguiled, desperate, but infatuated English husband kneeling at her feet. The three acts in between have illustrated, in terms emphatic and easy, the clash between Eastern and English temperaments and ethics. The marriage of Harry Anderson with the half-cast beauty Daisy is 'an international episode'; the love between Daisy and George Conway conscience-stricken on his part, unscrupulous on hers, is a deft piece of romantic magazine literature; both are tough, serviceable strands for tethering attention. I noticed on comparing the play as performed with the published text that a good deal of the crudity, as I supposed, of the preparation was due to cutting, but—and here is the proof that Mr Somerset Maugham knew his business thoroughly—such omissions left the situations, so far as the incurious were concerned, solid and striking.

He has drawn Daisy well, and she is well acted. The characteristic which he wisely shows from the moment she comes on the stage is her insensibility to the claims of loyalty and straightforwardness. So far it would be gross partiality to describe her as Oriental; it is only the lengths she is presently prepared to go in order to satisfy her passion for George, namely, her easy consent to the removal of her husband at the suggestion of her mother and her Chinese ex-lover, and her gradual transformation from a bewildered, pitiable little adventuress of the common type to something harder, more primitive, conscienceless and simple, which illustrates the theme of the play, that East is East and West is West and never the twain shall meet—except to their mutual discomfiture.

The most admirable invention in the play is Daisy's grotesque, ever-present nurse, who turns out to be her mother, most vividly played by Miss Marie Ault. She represents the Oriental conception of loyalty, unscrupulous towards all except the object of devotion. The effect of the narrow yet philosophic tenacity of this hideous old woman and of grim, placid Lee Tai Cheng, Daisy's ex-master, is to make the fervid emotional passions of the Europeans seem flimsy and childish. Mr Somerset Maugham has not drawn George well. He has not been sufficiently interested in him. As I have taken the opportunity of observing whenever I have criticised one of his plays, the angle from which he sees deepest into life and character is cynical. He has, for obvious reasons, represented George as the high-minded, generous English gentleman, who is miserable at having yielded to his passion for his friend's wife; but the conventionality of the result shows that the dramatist's sympathies lie elsewhere. The scene in which George yields to the passion of Daisy is an almost comic reversal of masculine and feminine parts: 'Don't, don't. Oh, this is madness!' . . . 'Oh, I've been here too long! Daisy, I beseech you let me go. . . .

I know how good and kind you have been. . . . My precious'—these exclamations wrung from the distracted George echo in my memory. Mr Maugham goes near to suggesting that George chucked Daisy for the uninteresting, eligible Sylvia Knox, but —unfortunately he boggles at this sensible and coherent conclusion, and Daisy's revenge is left on our hands as a mere piece of misguided vindictiveness.

FOR SERVICES RENDERED

1932

THIS IS THE best play Somerset Maugham has written, and it is thoroughly interpreted. All critics agree that it is admirably acted; all play-goers who have seen it are enthusiastic on that score and, if they are aware that there is such a thing as dramatic technique, over the skill of the dramatist. Various opinions have reached me from various quarters. Some of these are sufficiently enthusiastic to satisfy me, in others admiration is tempered by dislike, but all agree that *For Services Rendered* is a remarkable play. And everyone says that it is 'grim'. This small word expresses approval in the case of the tough-minded and distrust in the mouths of the tender-minded. Where there is unanimity between these two types of play-goers the critic would be rash who rejected their common verdict. I am certainly not going to argue against it. Personally, I like 'grim' plays, and 'grim' novels, provided they are not distorted by spiteful arrogance or written out of disgruntled vanity; and anyone acquainted with Mr Somerset Maugham's best work in drama and fiction knows that such a play as this springs straight out of his own vision of the world. It is not that of an amiable man who gives human nature the benefits of doubts; it is not that of a man whose indignation is heightened by a desire to redeem mankind, and it is not that of an idealist bitterly disappointed in human-

nature. It is the work of a man who now and then has been
angry with people for not having the honesty to admit facts
which stare them in the face, but has kept that anger on ice long
enough to turn it into an instrument of his searching contempt.
What are the facts that this careful, cold, considered anger
exposes? I shall not tabulate them for a good reason. If I were
to write them down in a list every reader would say at each
item, 'Of course! I never denied that'. Nevertheless, it is quite
a different matter when their truth is vividly projected in a
picture of life. Then, the very people who would assent with
the most off-hand alacrity to each statement are precisely those
most likely to boggle at the truth of the picture. Indeed, it is
against this comfortable, comforting faculty of admitting anything and feeling nothing, that the play is directed. The villain
of the piece is not exposed till the last moment; and during it
he is so artistically concealed that it is possible that many
spectators leave the theatre without recognising him for what
he is. I say, artistically, because once you have grasped the
significance of the play, his exposure is the more complete (as
in the case of Ibsen's best characters) through his having
appeared in art as he does in life, his nature concealed by conventional rectitude and platitude, muffled up in good-humour
and apparent common-sense. The country solicitor and father
of the family in the play (excellently acted by Mr C. V. France,
and all the better, I suspect, from the actor's not being completely
aware of the devastating implications of his part) is its villain,
or rather the embodiment of what the play exposes. What Mr
Ardsley embodies is an attitude which in private-life is often
called balance and in politics back-bone. It is an English quality,
infuriating to the truthful and the despair of those who do not
believe in 'muddling through'. It is the elderly Ardsleys who
never have any difficulty in saying 'yes' to wars, or in accepting
their consequences with a firm placidity. During wars they
sometimes make fortunes and they always give sons, regretting
that they are unable to do more themselves than act occasionally
as special constables. Their patriotism is absolutely reliable;

but they are incapable of the smallest effort to grasp the difference between their own point of view and that of those who did not share their immunity. They are idealistic for others and practical for themselves; their hearts would be in the right place if they had any. They find suffering tolerable to contemplate and excuse and quench complaints as hysteria or crying for the moon. They think it foolish to meet trouble half-way, which means they ignore the troubles of those nearest them, and *a fortiori* of those they do not see. They are generally hearty men and, while well off, hospitable. Their confidence rests on an hypothesis that the worst never happens to them, and as long as it doesn't 'the old country is sound at bottom'. Therefore they cannot also help believing that any remedial measure which might possibly injure them, *must* ruin everybody completely. They seem steady as rocks, but threatened with bankruptcy they often shoot themselves, which shows that it is not courage that supports their genial equanimity but a method of looking at life. This method is to shut the eyes to anything painful until it is too late to remedy it. Now the art of shutting eyes requires cultivation, (Men, unlike puppies, are born with them open), and during the war it was an absolute necessity for those who kept the home fires burning to acquire it in perfection. Consequently, to-day, the most finished adepts belong to that particular generation—still too much with us. No task more salutary could be undertaken at the present time by a detached observer of human-nature than that of exposing Ardsleys; and dramatically there is no better way of doing so than by exhibiting them as denying with practical friendly effrontery (1) the obligations of their recent idealism, (2) bravely making light of the sufferings physical, mental or financial the war has entailed upon others. This is exactly what Mr Maugham has done, and with that artistic coldness which alone can make the blood boil.

But do not make the mistake of several of his ablest critics of supposing that every fact about others to which this Ardsley blandly and firmly ignores ought to have been directly attributable to the war itself. No: the play is about Ardsleys not merely about services rendered and ignored. This Ardsley 'carries on', still he is left unwittingly at last with a dying wife, a crazy sex-starved daughter, a blind embittered son on his hands, and the responsibility for a war-hero's suicide on his conscience, if that conscience did not distinguish so clearly between what is his business and other people's, between homage to patriotism and the obligation to help patriots. The final climax of the play is one of the best engineered and most shattering explosions of wilful smugness I have ever witnessed on the stage: when Mr Ardsley over his tea-cup makes a brief speech in the key of the concluding tableau of *Cavalcade* and his youngest daughter, the one scatheless creature attached to him bolts from the house, as from a city of destruction, into the arms of a rich elderly married man whom she neither loves nor trusts. It is the only alternative.

The play opens in a large and pleasant garden belonging to this leading solicitor in a quiet country town. He has three daughters and a son. The family and their guests have been playing tennis. We are put in touch with the situation in a masterly fashion. Young Ardsley was blinded in the war, one of his sisters lost her fiancé in the war, and the other married in a moment of hero and uniform worship a rough tenant farmer, a heavy drinker and a coarse-grained sensualist. The youngest was only a child when these things happened. Their guests that afternoon are a young ex-naval officer who set up a garage in the town with his bonus money, and a rich elderly man and his silly-hard wife, a divorcée, who are the temporary tenants of the neighbouring Manor House. In the course of a perfectly natural dialogue we gather the position of all these people *vis à vis* each other. The blind son has taken refuge in a brooding and bitter self-control. (Perfectly played by Mr Hardwicke.) The bereaved daughter has taken refuge in self-sacrifice and has apparently resigned herself to being for life a devoted nurse to her brother and a mother's help. The married daughter is making the best of the bed she has to lie on and conceals as much as possible from herself and her family the misery of her misalliance. The youngest child sees no prospect in front of her but withering on the stalk like her eldest sister. The sailor's garage business has been going badly and a crash is inevitable unless he can borrow say £200. He knows that it is no use appealing to his friend and solicitor, and we soon understand why. He fails to get a loan from the rich elderly man, his last hope, who has already cast an amorous eye upon the youngest Ardsley girl, and who is prepared to give her the best of times, and to settle £20,000 on her if she will come away with him. (He does buy her in the next act, as bait, a pearl necklace worth £500.) In the first act there is a hint, too, that the bereaved mateless daughter whom her father finds it so convenient to conceive as cut out for a 'saint', is in love with the ex-sailor. In the Second Act all these potentialities are developed. The principal line that development follows is the fix in which the ex-commander of a destroyer finds himself, and the frantic un-returned passion he has inspired in Ardsley's eldest daughter Driven to desperation he has, after a definite warning from his Bank, tried to stave off creditors by drawing stumer cheques; driven to desperation, in an agony of embarrassment, she offers him herself and the £1,000 which belongs to her. We watch her first breaking down hysterically while playing chess with her brother.

With that trenchant benignity which marks treatment to all who have served England, although a prosecution is inevitable, thanks to his D.S.O. the naval officer may get off with six months in the second division. Ardsley's comment to his blind son is that 'Collie was a good officer but a bad man of business', but when the son replies that that would make an excellent epitaph for Collie's tombstone, Mr Ardsley is characteristically shocked. Between Act II and III Collie Stratton shoots himself. When the blind Sydney trembling with ice-cold passion declares that if there is ever another war, he will go out into the street and shout 'Bunk, bunk, bunk', his father's reply is, 'I'm sure my boy that when the time comes you will do your duty'.

Ardsley's favourite maxim is 'don't jump your fences till you come to them'—precisely, go on ignoring that popular feeling about war has changed. That dog won't fight again. The Ardsley's of every country believe that they are only up against a lot of washy weak pacifist sentiment. Nothing of the kind. The feeling is deep enough, If 'the war to end war' proves a fiasco, in every country there are many who will be willing, since death and disaster are inevitable, to try if civil-war won't do the trick.

The curtain descends upon the old order looking up startled from his tea cup, by the surprising bitterness of his son and by his daughter, who imagines herself engaged to the man who has just committed suicide, crazily singing the first two lines of God Save the King. Anyone who suspects himself or herself of in any respect resembling Ardsley should go—if only to find out. They can be sure of a thrilling entertainment.

NOEL COWARD

1934

HIS MAJESTY'S THEATRE is packed. The last time I *remember* having been there—for plays and entertainments are apt to pass from my mind more completely than books—it was also packed. Then *Bitter Sweet* was filling that enormous theatre. I enjoyed it; I wept—for I am not one of those who obstinately refuse to be led to the fountain of easy tears. It is a mistake not to enjoy sentiment; criticize it afterwards if you will, but it is stupid to withdraw yourself as though obvious pathos defiled. Pathos is one of the strong colours on the dramatist's palette; Shakespeare's pathos is often barefaced and laid on very thick.

What an astonishing man Noel Coward is! Never was a man more completely 'of the theatre'. Composer, dramatist, producer, actor, and, if I am not misled by certain touches, also designer for the stage. The spirit of his own fancy pervades everything.

> I am the batsman and the bat,
> I am the bowler and the ball;
> The Umpire, the Pavilion cat,
> The roller, pitch and stumps and all.

So the author of *Conversation Piece* might almost boast—ignoring for the moment that he could not have attained his end without the light, delighting humour and delicious birdlike voice of Mlle Yvonne Printemps. And what an astonishingly psychological *chef* he is! He knows exactly what ingredients will—first of all—mix; then what mixture will appeal to the public palate at a particular moment. Those ingredients must be fresh and yet familiar. If they are too fresh they will puzzle: 'What's this? Is it nice or nasty? I must ask someone else.' A playwright cannot fill His Majesty's night after night if he sets an audience talking to itself like that. On the other hand, if the flavours are too familiar, even if they give pleasure, the public won't be content. They will be uneasy, and when they talk about the entertainment afterwards, before they praise it and say 'Go, go', they will endeavour to convey that they are not behind the times, and that there was nothing new in it for them.

The explanation of the reluctance in some quarters to pay due tribute to Mr Noel Coward's extraordinary cluster of gifts—and to his equally remarkable and sensitive intelligence—is that he so often approaches his themes from a psychological *chef's* point of view when inventing a dish. They overlook that other part of his endowment, his unerring sense of what ingredients will blend— his artistic sensibility.

In *Conversation Piece* the ingredients are the Regency, Brighton, and a very old appealing situation: the little girl who falls in love with her elderly guardian, he having put aside the idea of winning the heart of youth. It is familiar—far older than *The Professor's Love Story*, but it is a theme on which pretty variations can be played. It is slighter than the theme of *Bitter Sweet*, which was so nicely timed. Then the young were wondering if they had not lost something in scrapping romantic love, and the older generation were quite sure that they had; and the latter had the intense pleasure of saying at *Bitter Sweet*: 'Look, that is the way *we* fell in love.' It was seldom true, but *Bitter Sweet* was pertinent criticism of Cupid's latest phase, and Mr Noel Coward's heart was in it.

In *Conversation Piece* there is no criticism of modern life. It is a theme for sentimental and visible decoration; it is adroitly taken advantage of. Love between youth and age is never stale. The Regency craze is over, and yet it is not stale. We still like to see women looking like crocuses or elaborate milk-cans; the spectacle is not too familiar or too strange. We all know Brighton and we all are aware of the 'sunny domes' of the pavilion and of the shades of Prinny and Mrs Fitzherbert behind the confusion of the asphalt parade. *Conversation Piece* is a pageant not too familiar and not too fresh; and at His Majesty's it is pretty indeed to watch. The piece is a brilliantly adorned, coloured, sentimental extravaganza. It sends up the spirits, though it is in danger at certain points of moving too slowly.

To test the *ensemble* of scenes and also the breadth of the acting I went again, a second time, to see it from the back of the dress-circle whence those things are better estimated. They passed that test magnificently. And I noticed this, that Mr Noel Coward's acting had gained in a night or two in assurance and succinctness and authority. He, the elderly guardian and ruined French aristocrat, has a difficult part to play. Composure is its keynote; monotony its danger. He achieves that elegant composure in gesture and movement which is absolutely necessary as a contrast to the *gaminerie* and gaiety of the delicious 'Yvonne', whose walk and graceful petulant awkwardness reinforces the child-of-nature note in the words she has to speak.

About the pictures which the play forms continually before our eyes—they are only 'anecdote pictures', but they are very agreeable and inspire indeed an astonished pleasure. It is odd—I should like some day to go into this—a picture which I would not look at on a wall gives me pleasure on the stage. Had I seen a painting which was a facsimile of, say, the tableau of the Regency party in Act II, I would not have given it a second glance, but on the stage it riveted me; perhaps because I knew that in a moment it would vanish and change, and because I was interested in the figures as human beings. Unconsciously in the theatre one applies standards which are different, not purely æsthetic ones. But one scene or rather one item in a scene, the sea-light beyond the sitting-room windows, seen through the graceful iron-work of the balconies of that yellow room, never ceased, even while Mlle Printemps herself was singing, to enter into my total pleasure.

But I must add a word or two about the story; Mr Noel Coward has sprinkled a little pepper over the sweetness of his dish. In the first place the aristocrat-guardian himself is also an adventurer. He intends to marry a girl he has picked up in a cabaret in France, to a rich Englishman and thus recoup his battered fortunes with a commission on the marriage. The

critical observer will not fail to notice the adroitness with which
the dramatist has leapt over the common-place after she has
declared her love for him. It is a near shave, but the pitfall is
just cleared. There is, for instance, the first kiss between them,
after which he stumbles blind and miserable to the door; and
she—as we anticipated—buries her face in her hands—for love
between them means ruin to both. But then, when she raises
her face, she suddenly skips into the merriest of triumphant
dances! That moment is brilliantly right. It is an example of
that quick adroit tact which enables Mr Coward to be sentimental without being flat. He has, too, one more surprise for us
up his sleeve, when we think all is plain sailing. The scene which
struck me as missing its mark was the ballet (for so it is) in the
garden, at night, after she has declared her love, and he has
become aware that he longs for her and for love; when he knows
that he cannot now without pain go on with his scheme of
marrying her to the young marquis. The idea of his watching, in
agony of mind, the roving lovers in the garden is dramatically
right; but to my mind the drama would have been more effectively conveyed had his movements *not* been those of the dancer
seeking in a ballet for his lost love, peeping into women's faces
and making the dancer's gestures of despair—if he had remained
a realistic figure; an elderly man, almost motionless beneath a
tree, an outcast in a garden of love.

I cannot criticize the music. The piece is full of pretty,
conciliating, titillating airs.

JAMES BARRIE

DEAR BRUTUS

1917

SIR JAMES BARRIE has 'a way with him'; what kind of 'a way' I hope in the course of writing to discover. Meanwhile, let me recommend *Dear Brutus* as an amusing and riveting entertainment.

Now, it is often worth a critic's while to keep his ears pricked while jammed in the cloak-room rush after a performance. It is the laconic comments of men to each other—before they rejoin their ladies in the lobby—that I have most often found instructive, especially comments of men who never (so one guesses) analyse their impressions except for practical purposes, and even then mistrustfully. Often such remarks contain the gist of criticism, and when not, they are still apt to be useful as aids to graduating that asinometer for measuring the public intelligence which no critic or playwright should be without. What I overheard last night may not seem of much value when quoted, but I instantly recognized its value to me. The dialogue was brief.

First dull middle-aged man, waiting for his coat and hat: 'Well, what did you think of it? Good?'

Second ditto: 'Yes, I thought it good. Anyway, it's something new.'

That's it, I thought; that's the right key, with modulations out of it into a more enthusiastic one, in which to pitch a criticism of this play. 'Something new.' The moment I heard those words I realized I had been reminded of what I might otherwise have forgotten to mention, namely, Sir James Barrie's originality.

It is easy to overlook Sir James Barrie's originality, partly because it lies in front of the nose, and partly because in another way he is the least original of gifted writers. His criticism of life contains nothing new; he does not even stick up passionately for the old; he does not clear up anything, or even confuse anything. His sense of values is that of the gentle mid-nineteenth-century novel (fairly sane, but very sentimental) and of the *Boy's Own Paper*. No one ever got fresh light on ways and means, or on morals, or on human nature, from him; only delightfully odd, slight, and sometimes surprisingly penetrating, confirmations of indulgent current judgments. Nobody ever came away from a Barrie play wondering if something in human nature, which they had thought was rather beautiful before, was not, after all, rather hideous, or what they had thought hideous was not really rather fine; no one ever came away convinced he saw the Devil's horns sticking up in an unexpected quarter of human experience, or noticing for the first time in a puddle the reflection of a star.

Of course, he is much saner than many people in whose heads a few modern bees buzz in a vacuum. He would never be guilty of the silliness of some enterprising intellects now in revolt. One cannot imagine him writing a novel or a play in which a soul was saved for ever by someone surprising another bathing, or in which a man who slit his sweetheart's throat in a fit of glorious disgust was held up to admiration, while a mildly selfish, conventional old woman was hunted down for pages as a vampire. Yet he is too soft to be a sound artist. Or, to put the statement positively, as an artist, the background which his arrangements in human nature—black and white and pink—demand, in order to justify them and set them off, is a nebulous one, implying that life is a romantic, tender, straightforward adventure, and, to be lived well, must be taken as such. It is not firmly apprehended enough, this philosophy, to be a faith in him; it is not make-believe either, but something (so I feel) betwixt and between.

The characters to whom his heart goes out are those he conceives as holding it with a more wholehearted simplicity than he can himself encompass; consequently, he writes about them at once very sentimentally and very penetratively. This is the secret of his adoration of youth (for youth has *the air* often of taking life on trust as a romantic adventure), of his capacity for

K

drawing young creatures, of his insight into them, and of the limitations of that delightful insight—which are very marked, to my mind. It also accounts for his happy touch in drawing old people, in whom there is often not exactly a second childhood but a second innocence, and granted a certain easiness of circumstance and heart, a disposition to make of life in retrospect a pretty, simple picture. The sympathy of such old people for the young is boundless, tender admiration—provided that the young consent to being figures in the picture and remaining in it; but woe betide if they do not!

Sir James Barrie's attitude towards youth in his writings strikes me as being a mixture between that of an old man, who no longer has any quarrel with life or his own desires, and that of a young girl. Crossjay, in *The Egoist*, is boyhood seen through Clara Middleton's eyes, and delightful Crossjay is, too. But those who have been boys themselves know that a good deal is left out of the picture, and not merely unaccommodating, harsh facts, but all sorts of virtues inextricably connected with them, almost all the growing principle, indeed, all the sap by virtue of which the creature becomes at last a being 'looking before and after'. A boy is not only a right little, tight little fellow, with nothing incongruous to him but an adorable affectation of premature manliness; he is a confused creature, ready enough to accept standards from his elders, trying them on, but having to retire perpetually into reserve, like a growing crab under a rock while it sheds its small shell; and a very uncomfortable, naked, helpless creature it feels until its new, larger one is hardened.

But Sir James Barrie does not like growth. He likes best people who do not grow up, who remain—even at an advanced age—boys and girls; in the static state of harmony with the world and guilelessness he conceives as characteristic of youth. Judging him as an artist, he strikes me in general as beautifully unshockable, most wisely indulgent; but there is one thing I think would shock him artistically—a youth who did not take an enthusiastic, trusting attitude towards the world, who was discontented, though not personally persecuted, sceptical, self-withdrawn, world-questioning, disillusioned. I cannot approve Sir James Barrie as a lover of youth, because I have never yet seen in his work that sympathy with pimpled and sullen spiritual gawkiness which, it seems to me, youth's true lover must also possess. Youth is essentially the thinking time. It is an enjoying time, too; but compare the process of thinking in later life with the really anxious, sensitive, bebothered search for understanding and sympathy characteristic of early years. Why, afterwards thinking becomes, in comparison a mere accomplishment and friendship an art, needing a little care and patience—like boiling an egg. It is no longer a crucial, personal experiment.

Sir James Barrie is pre-eminently a dramatist who deals with youth and its charm. What I miss in him—in that capacity—is disinterested sympathy with, and interest in, the questing, crude, spring-like temper of growing beings, which has the beauty, but also drizzling, uncomfortable rawness, of actual spring-time. His magic, his great charm for the public, lies precisely in his depicting youth and age only in the light of the autumnal glow of elderly fancy. His is a world in which the most jarring note of all would be the one which hums through nearly everybody's twenties—the pathetic, bitter conflict between the young and old generation. He stops his ears to that—and the public love him for it.

Eighteenth-century critics used to praise writers for their 'inventiveness'; we go on about 'creative' power—a different thing. Sir James Barrie has the most surprising and easy 'inventiveness'. At every turn he can supply some ingenious, entertaining incident to carry on his story. This faculty works so spontaneously that it gives an air of extreme lightness to his best plays. He seems to have made a play out of nothing. But that is only because the machinery of narration is so supple that he has time to be amusing and apparently inconsequent by the way. Compare him with others who attempt the light fantastic. How stodgy and how over-solemn they appear when they introduce the playful supernatural! At the beginning of this play there is a delightful piece of inventiveness concerned with the butler, Matey; but I will not spoil pleasure by exposing the surprise.

A number of guests gathered together for midsummer week 'because they all have one thing in common'. What that is, they are desperately curious to know. They cannot guess. Their host is the queerest old creature, of unimaginable age and uncanny agility. He is called 'Lob'—no one calls him anything else. He is not human, but he has a comfortable little house and a butler, and there is a mischievousness in him, a *méchanceté*, which makes one doubtful if he *is* a benevolent being. He talks tenderly to his flowers (which seems amiable), but his attitude towards human beings is marked by a Puck-like detachment and, one suspects, a Puck-like contempt. This being is most admirably imagined; our credulity is amused, never strained, and the part is most admirably played by Mr Arthur Hatherton.

It turns out that what these people have in common is the feeling that if only they had another chance they would make a better thing of life than they have. 'Lob' has on midsummer night the power to give them that chance and teach them the lesson that most of them would have in any case been just the same as they are now. Only two of them had really had 'bad luck'—an artist who has taken to drink, married to a wife who is harsh to him. (Mr Gerald Du Maurier gave a perfect representation of this character, and Miss Hilda Moore was excellent.) The fault in the case of the others was not in Fate, but in themselves.

The philanderer, when in the magic wood, goes on just the same, only he is married then to his flame and makes love to his wife—while both women behave inversely just as they did before. The tender, elderly, optimistic, happily married man, whose only trouble is that he fancies he might have written a great work, does nothing but hop about in the wood playing the flute. Matey, who thought that if he had taken a clerkship in youth he would have been an honest man, appears as a robber financier, and the hard, aristocratic lady—who had been merciless to his pilfering in the house as butler—adores him in the magic wood as a superman.

The 'invention' of the return to ordinary consciousness—one after the other in each other's presence—is delightful. There are fine touches—such as the fact that the only person who does not go into the wood is the affectionate, simple-hearted wife of the optimist. His proposal to her when in a half-waking state is charming, and so is her reply. He is the only one who had been faithful to a vague recollection of his love; but he had been quite happy with only that. 'Yes, but it is not such a compliment as I thought it was', she says rather sadly.

The comedy of love-making outside the marriage ring is deliciously satirized in the philanderer, who becomes kinder to his wife in proportion as the temporary mistress of his heart is kind to him. In fact, though the theme is old, the play is, as the gentleman in the cloakroom said, 'good, and, at any rate, something new'.

PLAYERS

SARAH BERNHARDT

1923

THE BEST CRITICISM of Sarah Bernhardt, and the finest tribute to her in English, is to be found in Mr Maurice Baring's *Puppet Show of Memory*, where she has a chapter to herself. I recommend this chapter to all who wish to recall or define her genius. 'The actor's art dies with him; but the rumour of it, when it is very great, lives on the tongue and sometimes in the soul of man, and forms a part of his dreams and his visions,' he writes, 'and we who never saw Rachel get an idea of her genius from the accounts of her contemporaries, from Théodore de Banville and Charlotte Brontë. Her genius is a fact in the dreams of mankind; just as the beauty of Helen of Troy and the charm of Mary Stuart whom many generations of men fell in love with. So shall it be with Sarah Bernhardt. There will, it is to be hoped, be great actresses in the future— actresses filled with the Muses' madness and constrained to enlarge rather than interpret the masterpieces of the world; but Providence (so economical, so generous!) never repeats an effect; and there will never be another Sarah Bernhardt, just as there will never be another Heinrich Heine.'

I only saw her act five times. On two of these occasions she walked through her part, acting with perfunctory languor and mechanical adroitness; suddenly turning on the *voix d'or*, as an organist might pull out the *vox humana*, and then letting go in a rapid exhibition of herself as tigress, tearing the words between her teeth and spitting them out again, as though we were a pack of fools (and I dare say we were) who had paid to see her tricks. She was, in fact, on those occasions the kind of actress her admirers, like Sarcey, feared she might become while touring the globe as one of the world's wonders. Although I concealed my disappointment the first time I saw her act, for fear it should be my own sensibility that was at fault, that disappointment was deep; and I read afterwards with enthusiastic assent Mr Shaw's criticism in *Dramatic Opinions and Essays*, in which she was compared most unfavourably with Duse.

But the next time, I saw the real Sarah—her performance as *Phèdre* shot far beyond mere excellence. Opinions were often divided about her acting in London in the 'nineties and later.

> Silver gilt will often pass
> Either for gold or else for brass,

and it happens not infrequently that the work of artists, which has value but still greater pretensions, is as much underrated by some as overrated by others. No doubt not a little of the acting Sarah Bernhardt showed us in this country was of the silver-gilt description, with the result that while the ignorant shouted 'gold', some of the discriminating cried 'brass'. But she also gave us the purest gold. If my ear can detect the ring of true metal, I heard it that night in *Phèdre*. In *Fédora*, in passages of her performance of *Hamlet*, too, I heard it again.

Mr Baring has recorded the significance she put into the scene in which Hamlet answers Polonius's question, 'What do you read, my Lord?' Hamlet was lying in a chair reading a book. 'The first *'des mots'* he spoke with an absent-minded indifference, just as anyone speaks when interrupted by a bore; in the second *'des mots'* his answer seemed to catch his own attention, and the third *'des mots'* was accompanied by a look, and changed into an intense but fugitive attention: something

> 'between a smile and a smothered sigh',

with a break in the intonation that clearly said, 'Yes, it is words, words, words, and all books and everything else in life and in the whole world are only words, words, words, words.'

I remember another moment of that performance which in imagination and intensity I never saw equalled by any other Hamlet.

When Hamlet runs his sword through the arras and, hearing a

body fall, thinks he has accidentally killed the king, she stood suddenly tiptoe, like a great black exclamation mark, her sword glittering above her head, and a cry, 'C'est le Roi!' rang in our ears, so expressive of final triumph and relief, that for a tingling second it seemed the play itself must be over.

The voice is the actor's most potent instrument of expression. All the papers in the world are striving now to recall Sarah Bernhardt's voice—its cooing, chanting sweetness, its feline violence, its thrilling clear whisper, its guttural cries of animal passion. She might have acted in the dark and have held us.

In addition she had a strange, frail, inhuman beauty, animated by an electric vitality; and though she could on occasion be insolently casual, offering us contemptuously 'her reputation instead of first-rate acting', yet throughout her long career she slaved at her art like one who can only with the utmost effort fulfil what he has undertaken. It was a very conscious art; you may even call it artificial. In the case of Duse you forgot that Duse was *acting*. Is that a greater tribute? It depends upon the part. In some parts it certainly is; while in suggesting beauty of character Duse was easily supreme. Sarah Bernhardt was always the actress as well as the part; at her best she was both equally. Consequently, she was at her very best in plays where the passions were expressed in a dramatic convention which does not attempt to compete with nature or to create the greatest illusion, but to interpret life on another.

When Sarah Bernhardt began to act, Racine's tragedy was held to be cold and monotonous compared with the work of the great romantics. It is thanks to Rachel and Sarah Bernhardt, more than to any literary critic, that modern taste has come to recognise in the alexandrines of Racine inflections as simple and delicate as Verlaine's, and to perceive, if not even to exaggerate, the expression of passion in his dramas; for after all he is not a Shakespeare. Frenchmen say that no actress ever spoke Racine's verse with more subtle and varied precision, or more musically, than Sarah Bernhardt; the foreigner was at any rate conscious of her perfect balance between the conventional and the realistic in such parts as Phèdre.

In her acting at its best she achieved what modern poets long to do—to express their own personalities with spontaneous freedom without losing the dignity and definiteness of a conscious work of art.

DUSE AND BERNHARDT

1924

DUSE IS DEAD, and this means that a unique kind of beauty has gone from the world, to live, not insecurely, but, alas! vaguely, as a tradition. Of the two great actresses of our times some preferred one, some the other. For my part I preferred the art of Duse to that of Sarah Bernhardt. It was less imposing, but more beautiful; it gave me emotions I valued more. Both actresses often transcended rather than interpreted their parts; and what they added was often more precious than the playwright's work. But the quickest way of suggesting the difference between their talents is to say that the art of Sarah Bernhardt made us first conscious of the beauty of emotions and passions, while that of Duse was a revelation of the beauty of human character. Her art was more personal; its effects more dependent upon subtleties and sincerities. When we left the theatre we felt as if we loved Duse herself, and that whatever she had been made to do and say in her part, she could not be very different from the character she had played; while in the case of Sarah Bernhardt we felt that what we had seen was the performance of a great actress.

To say this is not (heaven defend us from such stupidities!), to deny art to Duse or naturalness to Sarah, but the naturalness of the latter was that of her part under the technical conditions of representation, and the art of the former to fill the part she played with the grace of her own sensibility and the profundity of her own emotional experience. She did it so perfectly that we ceased to be conscious of those technical conditions. Any crowd could see that Sarah was a great actress, but not every member of it could be aware of the significance of that revelation of character which Duse put into her gestures and intonations. That revelation could be either one of exquisitely light

gaiety or of that pathos—the most touching pathos of all—which
strives, while longing for sympathy, to shield others from
realizing suffering too vividly.

A performance by Duse was apt to be a most devastating
criticism of the play, for her acting suggested many more
poignant and delicate things than the dramatist had put into
his situations. When her part lacked depth she supplied it,
while it remained of course shallow elsewhere. Sarah, on the
other hand, by the energy and adroitness with which she acted
up to the last limits of her part, would often redeem by sheer
passion a dramatist's tinsel.

I return to my original contrast, that the difference between
their talents was that the great Italian actress excelled in revealing beauty of character, the great French actress in revealing
the beauty of human passions. Several interesting results might
be expected to follow, and the careers of both corroborate them.
Sarah Bernhardt excelled in poetic tragedy; Duse's interpretation of realistic drama was far more delicately and profoundly
moving. If you saw her in plays like *La Dame aux Camélias* or
The Second Mrs Tanqueray, you asked yourself: 'What would
she be in a play in which the words and the dramatist's conception of her part were worthy of such acting!' Yet authoritative
criticism declares that then she was far from being her best; her
'Cleopatra', for instance, was not, it is said, a great achievement.
Sarah, on the other hand, was at her supremest in *Phèdre*. Such
parts did not permit of that delicate infiltration of Duse's own
personality into them, which was her own fine art upon the
stage, making lovely what was crude and significant what was
cheap.

In London last summer we saw Duse fill the part of the
mother in *Cosi Sia*, a monotonous part which could only lead
the most lamblike to the fountain of easy tears, with a delicate
variety of profound emotion, which changed every minute; a
wind of grief which rose to despair and sank to resignation. It
was a creation which suggested that, when genius interprets,
the dramatist's task might be merely to provide a finger-post,

leaving the actress to find her own way and to decide where to linger and where to hasten. We saw her, too, in another play in which the dramatist had been by no means content to be a finger-post—in *Ghosts*. Mrs Alving she turned into a sweet queen of sorrows, exercising by the very sweep of her dress and the delicious pleading of her hands, all battling, dun, northern harshness from the play.

From the nature of her talent she was free from the commonest faults of the actor—exaggeration, false emphasis. She excelled in reticence and minute fidelity; but it was always the reticence of a singularly thoughtful nature, though her part might be that of a flamboyant, thick-skinned thruster like Magda, and her fidelity was ever fidelity to herself. The nature of Sarah Bernhardt's talent, on the other hand, led her readily into the faults of the rhetorician in literature, who cares more for the forceful expression of emotion than for genuine expression. Blaze and amaze she always could in the hands of a rhetorical dramatist who did not distinguish, but for the perfect exhibition of her art she needed the work of Racine. Two things I wish I had seen. Duse when she played Juliet at an age not far in advance of Juliet's age, and her Desdemona; that part which is a pure and empty oval, asking for that beautiful variety Duse could supply.

Doubtless it was because her parts were *part* of her that she wore herself out so soon.

MRS PATRICK CAMPBELL

IT IS HARDLY worth-while to give an account of *The Matriarch*
which has already been running a considerable length of
time. Moreover it is not a bad play; but the plot is complicated without reflecting the complexity of life, and the dialogue
is without surprises or distinction. Yet it has one great merit:
it shows off a small segment of Mrs Campbell's talent. I wish
I could say that it exhibited its orb, but that would be a magnificent compliment and it deserves nothing of the kind. Still, the
slip of the full moon it does reveal is so bright, that it is well
worth the while of amateurs of acting to go to see *The Matriarch*.

The play gives her opportunities for displaying her gift for
comedy character construction. Passages of it also need her
natural and astonishing vehemence: no living actress can represent so well upon the stage the domination of a temperament.
She has to be an elderly jewess who becomes an old woman in
the course of the play, and to fill the part with unflagging
vitality. Thick-skinned kindness; the courage which comes
from revelling in life to such a degree that even disaster has
something exhilarating in it; and two passions, a Hebraic desire
to increase and multiply and a fierce egotistic devotion to her
numerous offspring—such is the character Mrs Campbell fills
completely. We first see her descending on a poor daughter
whom she has neglected for six years on account of her unsatis-
factory and barren marriage with a gentile. The girl knows only
one way to win back her elemental parent's good-will is to bear
a child; so she adopts a baby-boy and pretends it is her own.
Her possessive triumphant adoption of the child, the lavish
delight in distributing all the good things brought down to
celebrate; her cooings over the cradle (we know that Mrs Campbell in that direction can rival the dove); the fluctuations from
her psalmist mood to preoccupation with food and back again;
the mixture of respect, forgiveness and wounding personal in-

difference in her manner towards the supposed 'mother'; above all the easy breadth of these gestures which suggest elemental ruthless temperament and devotion of this massive, gawdy, tough, soft, slovenly, energetic, 'mother in Israel', are a delight to behold. That is the prologue. The first act exhibits her match-making with a blunt persistence and her imperturbable though surprised acceptance of failure in that line. In that act, too, we gather that it has been her indomitable will to greater and greater family prosperity which has landed the whole clan in bankruptcy. In the second act we watch her thoroughly enjoying grappling with misfortune; packing and planning, scolding and comforting. In the last act the focus of interest shifts (to the regret of amateurs of acting, though it is the point of the play) from the matriarch herself to her granddaughter who promises to reveal similar propensities. I have only two faults to find with this admirable performance: occasionally Mrs Campbell drop-ped the Jewish habits of enunciation and slipped back into uttering her vowel sounds in her natural manner and (this of course is the dramatist's fault) she speaks too many crudely 'funny' lines. The repeated misuse of idioms 'I have a tooth to pick with you' etc. depresses those whom it does not exhilarate.

Mrs Campbell's art has two roots. The one has enabled her to excel in refined poetic tragedy and even in those parts, such as Mélisande, which demand a dying langour and strange aegri-tude of passion. (Some may remember Mrs Campbell's perfor-mance with Sarah Bernhardt as Pelléas and how she seemed such stuff as dreams are made of.) While her other gifts seem rooted in the instincts of an Italian peasant; she has therefore always excelled in parts in which the veneer of convention is broken by uncontrolled impulses, and the seriousness of passion interrupted by the broad comedy of nature or a sudden harsh matter-of-factness. Mr Shaw of course took full advantage of her sympathies with uncultivated emotion and expression in writing the part of Eliza Doolittle. And it was this combination of antagonistic sympathies which made her first performances of Hedda Gabler so unforgetable. It enabled her to convey the

L

romanticism of Hedda, her not altogether vulgar detestation of the ignobly humdrum, and also to do magnificent justice to the egotistic drive in that unpleasant but pitiless pitiable young woman. Hedda, you remember, has 'danced till she is tired'. She considers herself not only *déplaccée* because she has married a humdrum bookish husband from the middle class, but in the world itself. She is as bored as Madame Bovary and boredom is a sensation which Mrs Campbell acts to the life. Above all she has a horror of 'nature' and especially of such relapses into natural life from civilisation as child-bearing entails. To herself her boredom and disgust are signs of aristocracy of spirit. And since her circumstances are too narrow for display, she falls back on inflicting petty humiliations on those near her and in her power. One moment of her acting I can reach perfectly now, though I saw it twenty-two years ago: her gesture, her intonation when Hedda pretends to mistake her Aunt Nora's new bonnet on a chair bought for the occasion, for the maid of all work's. It seems a little thing, but it was perfection, conveying in all its natural ugliness the deliberate desire to wound, allowing even just as much of that intention to be visible as would thrust the humiliation deeper, but keeping it sufficiently casual to make it impossible for the old lady to take offence.

The last time I saw Mrs Campbell in the part the production was a failure, very unlike the one which Mr Granville Barker supervised in 1907. She knew the play was in the doldrums, chose her own *tempo* independently of the other actors, and though she still recorded Hedda's contempt, Hedda's boredom perfectly, she played the big moments with a casual virtuosity which only showed up the inadequacy of the rest of the cast, without transmitting much emotion to the audience. Perhaps I was unlucky in the night I saw her then. But when I first saw her she managed to suggest along with all that is raspingly unpleasant and meanly tigerish in Hedda, something of the beauty of a ship, its white sails trembling, on a mud bank. Just as vividly as her Hedda Gabler those who saw Bjornson's *Beyond Human Power* probably remember her performance in that play. Until the very last moment of the play when she totters from her bed into her husband's arms she is lying down, an invalid suffering from some obscure paralysis and inveterate sleeplessness, full of queer delusions of the senses, premonitions, fears, but united to that husband by an unusual affection. How easy it is in such a part to overdo the morbid querulousness; to make monotonous the appeal to sympathy! She was perfect, with a grace which never detached itself from the realism of the sick bed, and her beautiful voice kept that play which is about a disastrous miracle, keyed up to that strange pitch in which strange happenings seem natural.

After seeing her in *The Matriarch* it is natural that any old playgoer should thus remember her in more memorable parts. Had I ever seen her fail? Yes, distinctly yes,—in a Barrie play, *The Adored One*. It was not the fantasy of it which baffled her, but there were moments when she was required to be very sweet and simple without being romantic. That note is not in her octave as an actress. When she had to sit shelling peas in a cottage window she could not help doing it with something of the air of Marie Antoinette playing at being a milk-maid in the Petit Trianon and to ask a lover quite naively if her seven children are not 'too many' when he asks her to marry him was quite impossible for her. You see there is absolutely no nonsense of that kind in Mrs Campbell. She cannot get away from basic emotional facts into a pretty world or a fairy world, or a purely kind world as an artist. Her escape from realistic emotion is straight into high romance. It was I think her firm grasp of emotional fact which made her 'Magda' certainly a better interpretation of the part itself than Duse's.

Duse was angelic, but Magda was not. She was a young woman who had knocked up against a few of the hardest facts in the world. and though she had to pretend when she returned to her friend's home she had not, they had left their mark upon her. Mrs Campbell whether in moments of merciful hypocrisy or self-defence became Magda to the life.

Why do I turn to reminiscences? Well, having just been

reminded how full of energy and how completely mistress of her art our finest actress is, I would fain suggest to some writer of plays that instead of following with entire independence his own genius he should take a hint and write a play for Mrs Campbell.

CHARLIE CHAPLIN

1923

MISS ELSIE CODD was some little time ago, and may be still for all I know, Charlie Chaplin's secretary. She has published an account of his methods of production. Eighteen hundred feet of a Chaplin film is the result of several months' hard work; 'his hardest work', she tells us, 'is not his own work in front of the camera.' I know nothing about film-production, but everyone will be prepared to believe that planning and scrapping (he is extremely exacting) is far the heaviest part of it, especially to one who has an unerring instinct for pose and movement.

I went to see the new Chaplin film, *The Pilgrim*, and it recalled to me Miss Elsie Codd's remark that during rehearsals Chaplin is perpetually exclaiming, 'Don't *act*.' He means, of course, 'don't *over-act*'; don't try too hard to be funny, pathetic, wicked, absurd; and his own pre-eminence is largely due to his being always, even in the most grotesque situations, in a sense, unexaggerative. I remembered, too, what he had written himself: 'Still funnier is the person in a ludicrous position who, in spite of it, refuses to admit that anything out of the ordinary is happening, and is obstinate in preserving his dignity.' (How exactly this describes his commonest and some of his best effects!) . . . 'That is why all my films rest on the idea of getting myself into awkward situations, so as to give me the chance of being desperately serious in my attempts to look like a very normal little gentleman. That is why my chief concern, no matter how painful the position I get myself into, is always to pick up my little cane at once, and put my bowler-hat straight, and adjust my necktie—even if I've just fallen on my head. I am so sure of this that I do not try only to get myself into these embarrassing positions, but I count on putting others also into them.' In *The Pilgrim* Charlie has no 'little cane'; he is an escaped convict who finds himself, by chance of course, impersonating a minister who is expected by the village community in the Far West. He has stolen the clothes of a bathing parson, the rest of his adventures follow automatically. Nevertheless, the 'fun' throughout is precisely of this kind; the continual pretence, when the most extraordinary and incongruous things happen, that nothing unusual or unbecoming has occurred.

There is, however, another element which is always contributive, not so much to our relish of particular scenes as to the effect the sum of ludicrous events makes upon us: I mean the perpetual contrast between complete helplessness, feebleness and absence of forethought in 'Charlie' and his indomitable adroitness in momentary crises. Here lies an opportunity for those who like to express their appreciation of this unpretentious artist in terms of refined speculation. If you want to see profundity in 'Charlie'; if you want to link up his art with serious imaginative creation, here is your chance. You can even penetrate if you like, at this point, down to a philosophy behind it.

The late Dan Leno, who was brother-in-art to 'Charlie', wrote his own biography. It is a sad little book, full of jokes, good and bad. In the course of it he says (I quote from memory), the Leno philosophy of life comes to this: 'I see the world as a football, kicked about by the higher powers, with me clinging on by my teeth and toe-nails to the laces.' It *is* a kind of philosophy; and one readily understood by all. Life, for the majority, easily bears that interpretation.

It appeals especially to the poor—at times to all of us. It is the philosophy of humility. That is why, like Dan Leno, 'Charlie' rouses sympathy so readily. His melancholy imperturbability, his perky recoveries, even his very transparent swagger, are, one and all, gestures expressive of a disarming humility. The famous 'cane' is symbolic of an unconquerable human aspiration towards dignity. There lies the fun—the hopelessness of that aspiration. 'I don't think I quite knew at first', he told us, 'how true it is that, for millions of individuals, a walking-stick marks a man as rather a "swell".' And so when I come shuffling on to the scene with my little cane and my serious air, I give the impression of an attempt at dignity, and that is exactly my object.' He knows the public likes to laugh and cry all in a minute. Whatever brevity may be to wit, it is certainly the soul of pathos, and 'Charlie's' pathos is conveyed in the briefest touches; a sudden fall of countenance, a shrug, a woeful attempt at a smile. Mr Chaplin knows we are in our hearts on the side of the unlucky against the lucky, of the poor against the rich, of the weak against the strong, of the kind against the unkind. 'Charlie' is therefore always ill-treated, always humiliated, and always—how consolingly—indomitable.

TWO ESSAYS

CENSORSHIP

1929

IN DISCUSSING this question of censorship I think we ought to keep before our minds that we are not a representative gathering in the ordinary sense. If we were we should be little use. We are people interested, for *various* reasons, in sex. I will not attempt to classify the different motives which have probably brought members of this audience together to study these questions, but I think I ought to say that I belong to that type of person who is not particularly interested in sex-problems but is here only in virtue of sharing a belief which is common to us all; that a real investigation of the sex instinct, and what mankind has made out of it, the history of love in all its forms, would probably throw more light on human nature and life than any other. When we have more light as to how human nature does, in fact, behave, we shall be in a better position to say how it *ought* to behave—or at any rate what to think of those who behave differently from ourselves.

Now such knowledge reaches us through two channels; through books, novels, and plays which are the peptonised experience of gifted people, sometimes called artists, and through scientific books. Although there is seldom now any barrier erected to prevent knowledge of any kind reaching us on other topics, we live in an age which, in different degrees in different countries and at different times, does put a sieve in front of the stream of facts and ideas upon sex matters which would otherwise reach us. What ought we to do about it? Or are our contemporaries right?

Let us proceed in this matter as though it were a sex-problem and discuss first *why* they behave in this way. They do so clearly from various motives. But the main one is I think this.

Men have always been afraid of their sex instincts. The

moment they became in any sense a community, let alone a civilised one, they embanked them between laws and customs, as though they felt that, let loose, those instincts would turn life into a swamp instead of irrigating and refreshing it. Some of those laws and customs have been exceedingly rigid and cruel; they have spoilt innumerable lives. Some men and women, especially the victims, have been aware of this at every period; but others have been aware of it too, many of them have said: 'Yes, I am sorry, but the banks though cruel to you are better than the swamp'. Other people won't even allow the banks to be examined. In so far, then, as opinion down the ages can be read in institutions and morals, it shows an instinctive fear than unless that strong interest is controlled it will destroy much that makes life worth living. Censorship is at bottom based on this age-old fear. At the back is the feeling that men and women are naturally too much preoccupied with sex, and therefore books and pictures which excite desire or books which tend to relax prohibitions ought to be suppressed. From time to time in history serious attempts have been made to do so. Of course it is utterly impossible to eradicate sex from art and literature, and everything that may excite desire. What is more, men have never stood for long any really drastic attempts in that direction. They have ignored and jeered at the purifiers. Still, the common sense of mankind does assent to some control being exercised over the manufacture of pornography, pictorial or verbal. To a certain extent they share with the Censorial party that vague apprehension that sexual appetite ought not to be continually stimulated. Now the curious thing about the situation is that the majority of Anti-censors and the majority of Censors both really want to compromise. The Censors don't really want to suppress works of art or prevent scientific enquiry; and the Anti-censors don't want the book-market or picture shops flooded with cheap pornography. But since many works of art and much good literature are powerful aphrodisiacs, the Censors don't know where to draw the line. When the Anti-censors say, why don't you suppress the Bible, Shakespeare, Titian, if you prosecute *this* book? they have no answer. They can only retort, But if you allow this sort of book to be published, how are you consistently going to prevent pornography being sold on every railway book-stall? The answer to that may be; but this book you are prosecuting has other important qualities. It is not written merely to excite lust. If you are going to make that the sole test where on earth will you stop? As Milton says, 'A fool will be a fool with the best book, yea, without book.'

A friend of mine once told me that he was travelling in a railway carriage full of undergraduates. One of them produced a photograph from his pocket which he handed round. He waited with some curiosity for it to reach his neighbour so that he, too, could see what was provoking so many signs of sly and salacious delight: it was a photograph of a Sir Joshua lady. This was an instance of a truth which the memories of all will probably confirm (I certainly might have deduced it from my own) that human beings in certain circumstances, will seek anywhere for something to stimulate their lubricity, and at certain ages to satisfy their curiosity. If the most rigid censorship was exercised over fiction and poetry in sex-matters, any poem or novel which went a step beyond the confines of the *Bibliotheque Rose* would be sought out for that purpose. In a novel which has recently appeared, which is a study of American adolescence, 'The Rampant Age' by Robert S. Carr, you will find his boy characters looking for stimulus in *The Idylls of the King*: 'and they pretty nearly do some hot necking in a couple of places, only they never quite make it', one of them remarks in criticising *Launcelot and Elaine*. You cannot keep the rooks out of the park by shutting the gates. Perhaps some would not wish even such facts to be known; such vulgarity is certainly not pleasant, but they have a bearing on this most vital question of freedom or discussion. If we are prepared to sacrifice the advantages or free-writing, we must be first certain that it is any use. Is anyone prepared to prosecute *The Idylls of the King*? Any law then which is aimed against pornographic books must be so framed that a book may be exempt from prosecution, if it can be shown that it has value, either as a work of art or of science or as a discussion of morals. Oddly enough it appears to me that such *is* the attitude if the law of England at this moment. You would not guess this from some recent prosecutions and verdicts, yet I believe this to be the case. I have said recently in print what I am about to say, but I wish to air this point again because I believe it to be an important one and since many of you are foreigners it may be interesting to you to know exactly how matters stand in England.

All proceedings against books are taken under Lord Campbell's Act, 'for more effectually preventing the sale of obscene books, pictures, prints and other articles.' When introduced in 1857 this Act was regarded as a salutary police measure. It aroused no interest among men of letters. (Monckton Milnes, was I think, the only literary man who took part in the debates and he supported it; the Athenaeum did not think it worth mentioning.) Its prime object was the suppression of a trade in obscene books and pictures which flourished particularly in Holywell Street. The vital clause of it runs as follows: 'If upon complaint there is any reason to believe that any obscene books etc. are kept in any house or other place, for the purpose of sale or distribution, and upon proof that one or more such articles has been sold or distributed in connection with such a place, justices may, upon being satisfied that such articles *are of such a character and description that the publication of them would be a misdemeanour and proper to be prosecuted as such*, . . . order them to be destroyed.' It is clear from the words I stressed that it is *not* sufficient to prove that a book is 'obscene' (whatever the legal definition of that word may be), in order to justify its destruction. The Magistrate must also be satisfied (A) that it is 'of such a character and description that the publication of it would be a misdemeanour'—that is to say that its publisher could be convicted before a common jury for issuing an 'obscene libel'; and (B) that the book is 'proper to be prosecuted as such'. Condition (A) is a clear direction to the magistrate not to condemn a book because he is shocked by it himself, but to ask himself what conclusion a jury would probably reach after hearing all that could be urged in the book's defence. The meaning of condition (B) is brought out—and it is vitally important—by the comments of the judges in the case of Regina *v.* Hicklin, the leading case which also furnishes Chief Justice Cockburn's definition of obscenity, now applies by magistrates to all books brought before them: namely, 'I think the test of obscenity is to deprave and corrupt those whose minds are open to such immoral influences, and in whose hands a publication of this sort may fall.' Once, then, a book has been shown to contain passages capable of corrupting minds capable of being corrupted it is taken for granted by magistrates that the book is condemned under Lord Campbell's Act. I speak as a layman, remember, but the comments of Lord Blackburn and Mr Justice Mellor, who were Chief Justice Cockburn's co-judges in that very case, suggest strongly that this is *not* the proper interpretation of the law.

What do the words 'proper to be prosecuted as such' mean? Lord Blackburn, who is regarded as one of the greatest English judges, after reading the section of the Act quoted above said: 'I think with regard to the last clause, that the object of the legislation was to guard against the vexatious prosecutions of publishers of old and recognised standard works, in which there may be some obscene or mischevious matter.

So whether the publication of the whole of the works of Dryden is or is not a misdemeanour, it would not be a case in which a prosecution would be "proper"; and I think the legislature put in that provision in order to *prevent proceedings in such cases*'.

It is clear then that in Lord Blackburn's opinion the words 'proper to be prosecuted as such' are not a necessary presumption of law from the finding that the work in question contains obscene matter, but a *separate* and *essential* condition inserted to safeguard from prosecution works which would *otherwise* come under Lord Campbell's Act. That is to say a provision for the protection of 'recognised standard works', i.e. works whose literary merit has been recognised. Mr Justice Mellor was also sitting upon the case; his comment goes, I think, further. It was that, in the case of books, the question whether any obscene matter in them brings them under the Act *is one of degree*, the object with which such matter is introduced being taken into consideration in determining that degree.

It is not an uncommon belief among elderly men in whose lives literature plays a subordinate part, that only 'old' master-pieces are of any importance to mankind. Lord Blackburn, in interpreting the words 'proper to be prosecuted as such' as a provision deliberately inserted in the Act to protect literature, forgot for the moment that it is still possible to add to the world's store of 'standard works'; and, with all respect to so eminent a lawyer, those words themselves afford no support for refusing to extend the same protection to contemporary works of merit. Mr Justice Mellor, I think, saw this. At any rate such a criticism is implied in his *obiter dictum* that the degree of obscenity permissible depends upon the nature of the work, a principle which is, by the bye, entirely destructive of Lord Cockburn's definition of indictable obscenity as anything which might corrupt anyone.

And what is the upshot? It is this: that if the Home Office when they cause a warrant to be applied for and the Magistrates when they hear the case, would consider, what in Law they are bound to consider, not only whether the books in question is obscene, but also whether the publication of it would properly lead to the prosecution of the publisher, and if they would give full weight to the *dicta* of the eminent judges who have inter-preted Lord Campbell's Act, we might then keep that Act as the salutary check it was intended to be upon traffic in porno-graphy, without any damage to literature, or without checking that perpetual pooling of knowledge and experience on which civilisation depends. But if they do not do this, then the law will fall into complete disrepute with reasonable people, and how bad that is for the moral sense of a community everyone with an inkling of statesmanship knows.

A last remark addressed to ourselves, 'Toleration and Liberty have no sense or use except as toleration of opinions that are considered damnable and liberty to do what seems wrong.' These are Bernard Shaw's words: We think Intolerance damnable; we must exercise some toleration towards it. Otherwise I am sure we shall never get along.

GOOD TALK

I

FRIENDS OF MINE in the country have sometimes been romantic enough to envy, so they tell me, the life I lead in
London—what they are pleased to call 'being in the heart
of things'; and I notice that what they have most often in mind
are social opportunities, chances of meeting people whose fame
makes them loom gigantic at a distance. They imagine that these
encounters, acquaintances, friendships, constantly afford me
the privilege of hearing wonderfully good talk. Well, I have met,
I do meet, many remarkable people, and, occasionally, I do hear
good talk—these things I reckon among my blessings; but they
are quite mistaken if they suppose that the occasions on which I
meet celebrities are usually those on which I hear the best talk.

Remarkable men and women often practise in company an
intellectual economy which would both surprise and disappoint
my country friends. Good talk arises out of happy situations, and
social occasions do not often produce these, even when the
company has been carefully selected with that hope. In the
first place, people seldom meet each other at dinners and in
drawing-rooms in moods sincere enough to stimulate the mind;
and, then, topics change too quickly for anyone to become
really interesting in them. People are so haunted by the fear of
being bored—or of becoming bores themselves, which is
worse—that the talk flitter-flutters about too restlessly. The man
or woman who shines most is the one who can say quickest
something passably amusing and pointful about anything.

II

I HAVE JUST read the last literary success. Rather rash; it would
have been safer to postpone doing so another three months.

Think of the immunity I have enjoyed hitherto! Everybody has been reading it, and if I have been asked once I have been asked a hundred times, 'What do you think of it?' Hitherto I have been able to turn, 'with the most civil triumph in the world', on my interlocutor, and reply truthfully that I have not read it yet. Now, however, I think I am fairly safe, several months have passed since the book's publication, and it is more likely that the same question will be put now about Mr Aldous Huxley's new novel; and in half a year's time I shall be able to read that also with impunity.

Of course I understand people wanting to know what others think about the books they have read; I often want to myself, but this zest for collecting bare statements of opinion from miscellaneous people puzzles me. 'Oh, I thought it *very* good,' 'Don't you think it is *rather* over-rated?' 'I enjoyed it *immensely*,' 'I was a *little* disappointed'—such comments do not seem worth collecting. They may express what was felt in each case, but they get one no further. The only possible reply is 'Oh!' What people seem to want from you is a neat little pellet of an opinion which can be flipped across a table, amusing if possible and repeatable. But I like the company of people who go hacking on at the same subject, even if that is only how to get a lawn in good order. If they go on long enough the subject is usually illuminated, but I notice that most people begin to get bored when I am just becoming interested, that I suspect I was born a bore myself; I prefer so distinctly the persistent to the hop-skip talker. I should very much like to hear two or three people discuss some new book of importance. Though I have heard such topic mentioned and dismissed hundreds of times, I have never heard such a discussion. After A has said he thinks it remarkable, B has said she enjoyed it enormously, C has said he thinks it much over-rated, A has gone on to say that he thinks future generations will take no interest in Shaw's plays, B that she detested *Lady into Fox*, C that he has been trying to re-read Henry James:—I don't call that literary conversation. It is not conversation at all. I seek two solid, long-winded, labyrinthine-minded, pertinacious bores with whom to discuss a book and who, when started on a subject cannot let it alone.

III

THE DISCREET bow-window in Ebury Street had not arrested my steps as I passed it, although I had *Conversations in Ebury Street* under my arm, and what should have been more delightful than to discuss the book with Mr George Moore himself? Yet I passed by. In the Mall I stopped and thought of returning, but felt again an inhibiting premonition. Of what? I will amuse myself, I said, in Mr Moore's own manner, and reflect very slowly and carefully upon this strange reluctance. Strange it was, for could I not have told him that I enjoyed many charming moments of literary pleasure while reading his book? Besides, had I been obliged to add that the criticism in *Conversations* had fallen far below the interest of the criticism in *Avowals*, was not Mr Moore the one author of my acquaintance who really could discuss with literary detachment what he had just written? In the course of colloquies, held in that very room, but colloquies certainly less urbane and Landorian than those recorded in the book, how often I have been struck by this surprising suspension of vanity in him just at the very point where men much less vain grew touchy. No craftsman ever forgot himself more completely in his work. Issuing late at night into Ebury Street I had often said to myself: 'Now I know where to go when I want to be reminded that the art of writing is important.'

I had an excellent excuse, too, for calling, for I appeared in *Conversations in Ebury Street* myself, though only, I am sorry to say, as the most negligible and futile of those interlocutors who attempted to put in a good word for the work of Thomas Hardy. Still, it was an excuse, and I wanted, too, to lodge a gentle protest at being made to say in the book that Landor's *Pericles and Aspasia* was the noblest work in the English language. And yet I had passed by! Why? Alas! I could not, in his own manner, luxuriously delay coming to a conclusion. No sooner had I asked

myself the question than pat the answer came: 'Yes, he *is* sub-
limely detached from his own stories, but what a bate he gets
into over his estimates of other writers.' There's the rub; I shall
have to listen to conclusions to which I cannot assent, while my
respect for the artist will withhold me from the relief of shouting,
'Bosh!'

In the book I had just been reading Mr Moore, Mr de la Mare,
and Mr Freeman are discussing what is the test of pure poetry,
and Mr Moore suggests that they should compile an anthology
What is his criterion? That a true poem is something which a
poet creates outside his own personality. Ignoring the vagueness
of such a test, for whatever a man creates is coloured by his
personality, it is clear that Mr Moore means that subjective
poetry is not 'true poetry', because Mr de la Mare next observes
that 'many of the most beautiful poems in the language would
have to be barred—Shelley's *Lines Written in Dejection in the
Bay of Naples*, for instance.' But it is when Mr Moore turns to
explaining where he will discover, and where he will not discover examples of true poetry, that his reader—and if the reader,
how much more his listener!—will find himself thrown into a
state of incredulous dismay. 'Milton does not abound in objective poetry, Pope still less, but we shall find several poems that
come within our definition in the *Songs of Innocence*, none, I am
afraid, in the *Songs of Experience*. Imagine a respectful visitor
many years his junior like myself, being left with a statement
like that on his hands! Milton a subjective poet! who with the
exception of few brief restrained references to his own feelings
as a blind and lonely man, is the most objective poet in English
literature, unless you range beside him—could my ears have
deceived me just now?—Pope or Dryden.

Mr Freeman is then made to remark: 'We shall find very
little in Keats,' and Mr de la Mare to add: 'I doubt if we shall
find anything' (I suspect this attribution); while Mr Moore
continues: 'Keats never attracted me ... I think of him too
frequently as a pussy cat on a sunny lawn.' Imagine your feelings
if a venerable writer, for whom you felt an admiration which

prevented you from being visited by the humour of Ham, told you that what strikes him most about Keats is a resemblance to a curled and comfortable cat!

What is the explanation? The reader will find it in the confession, recurring in Mr Moore's later personal works, that he has lost the power of reading. I doubt if he ever possessed it. On page 175 you will find a reference to a certain Augustus. We are given only one remark of his, but, as in the case of the one recorded utterance of Juliet's nurse's husband, it makes us wish to know more of Augustus. Whenever Mr Moore used to expound a general idea, Augustus after listening to him, invariably asked: 'What about the poor chap in the café?'—for it was his joke to assume that Mr Moore was entirely café-educated. Substitute conversation-educated, and there is much point in the joke of Augustus. Now education by conversation leaves a good many gaps. Nothing is more characteristic of Mr Moore than his discovering the Bible and *The Sentimental Journey* when he was past sixty, and his amazement at the density of a world which had not drawn his attention to their merits. He has an independent, whimsical, creative mind, and the truth is he has always read to stimulate his own talent. The writer who helps him most at the moment is consequently exalted above all others. At one time it was Landor; some years back it was Flaubert. This is, of course, not only legitimate but wise in a creative writer, but it is not a proceeding which trains the critic, who must yield himself to an author and not follow his own fancies across the page, or hunt for corroborations of his own literary methods in a book. Mr Moore laughs at me for being anxious about his literary education, and for writing 'a long, pathetic letter', urging the merits of Thomas Hardy. I am sure the pathos was not misplaced. He changes his view of authors when his own work takes a new direction. He once dismissed Stevenson as merely the smartest young literary buck in the Burlington Arcade; now he speaks of his 'radiant page', for Mr Moore happens to be now more interested than he was in the craft of constructing sentences. He has read Thomas Hardy in the spirit in which he read Newman, when he read the Newman in order to discover that no Catholic could write. Of course Newman is a good writer. But Mr Moore discovered some weak sentences in the *Apologia* and cried: 'There you are!' The results of this method are naturally surprising. I might apply it with the same results to Mr Moore, himself, to Pater, to Landor. I recollect an unfortunate sentence or two in 'The Confessions of a Young Man'—one comes back to me, about a piano leaning its melodious mouth towards a lady; Pater was not happy when he described Marius as being 'always as fresh as the flowers he wore,' a phrase more suitable to a society paragraphist; Landor's monumental skittishness is often utterly unworthy of him. Mr Moore, is, of course, absolutely without literary snobbishness. In this book he draws attention to a delicious passage in *Agnes Gray* where one vulgar little girl appeals to her sister to bear her out that she looked beautiful at the ball. 'Middling', replies the younger. We are grateful to Mr Moore for pointing out the delightful quality of that bit of dialogue, but when he goes on to declare that *Wuthering Heights* is poor compared to the novels of Anne Brontë, gratitude is not what we feel.

IV

I AM EXCEEDINGLY fond of controversy, not as a participant, but as a spectator. Indeed, I have never taken part in a dispute which was long enough to be called a controversy. My own exploits in that direction have never amounted to more than a brief blow, parry, and counter-blow, but I have watched others at the game; I imagine that I have learnt something about the noble art of self-defence. One's method should vary with strength of one's case and the character of one's opponent; that is the basic principle. For instance, suppose you have an unanswerable point to make, and this point, though it does not cover the whole of your case, is the most central one in the controversy, the character and gifts of your adversary should make you decide whether it is wiser to confine yourself to that single point, or whether you had better go for him all round and try to finish him up completely. (I am taking for granted that on all other points except the central one you have not such an immediately convincing case). It will also depend upon his character and gifts how far it will be prudent to attempt to show that he is a coxcomb, an idiot, an ignoramus or an ignominious person. It is unsafe to stray beyond your best point when you are dealing with an adversary of great mental agility. He will meet your weaker points, and pass over, as comparatively unimportant, your vital contention. He may indeed succeed in answering your minor arguments so well that the world at large will get the impression that the fight was drawn on 'points', when in reality he ought to have been counted out.

I know it requires great self-control not to caper about triumphantly after you have delivered a knockdown blow. Yet the more exuberantly triumphant your war dance round the prostrate body, the more likely are you to lay yourself open to a counter-blow, and the more delighted the spectators will be at seeing the tables then turned against you. And if you kick him when he is down, then, if he is a wily controversialist, he will instantly revive; his spirits will rise, and his wit, if he has any, will be displayed to the delight of all beholders. If, on the other hand, you have a weak case, you cannot do better than to lead off by being insulting. This may make your adversary lose his hair, and, forgetting he has the best case, he will perhaps turn the argument into a scrap in which you may be able to hold your own. But, if you have the best case, it is folly to let him stray away from that case into personalities.

V

IN A BOOK on spectres by Le Loyer, written in 1586, I came on the following passage:—

Of all the common and familiar subjects of conversation that are entered in company, of things remote from nature and cut off from the senses, there is none so ready to hand, none so usual as that of visions of spirits, and whether what is said of them is true.

It is the topic that people most readily discuss and on which they linger the longest because of the abundance of examples, the subject being fine and pleasing and the discussion the least tedious that can be found.

The same might be said of conversation to-day, only perhaps all would not agree that such conversations are 'the least tedious.' If not tedious, they are at any rate sometimes embarrassing; one is left with such startling statements on one's hands. Still more inexplicable than the spiritualistic wonders retold every day, is the way in which people take them. One dines out; one sits next to a lady whose aunt has seen a table levitate to the ceiling, and a medium walk out of one top-storey window and in at another. The lady herself has been to a necromancer in Bond Street, who has told her things about herself which he could not possibly have known by natural means, and others about her future which she is convinced will come true.

This starts off a man at the other side of the table telling, with impressive reserve, a story about a friend to whom a little grey woman appeared one night warning him that he must never leave the country—his friend thought nothing of it, but he went down on the *Titanic*. One then asks the lady if she has sat with her aunt's medium, and discovers not only that she has not done so, but does not even know his name. Fancy having had within grasp the chance of seeing a man walk on air and not seizing it! What is flabbergasting is the casual way in which people take experiences which ought to shatter that whole framework of reason to which we trust whenever we turn to the right to go out of a door on the right. If one evening a necromancer drew the moon out of the sky for me, and it turned out to be a flat silver platter about the size of an offertory plate—this would not be a whit more disconcerting than seeing a man walking upon air—I should be beside myself until I had assimilated the occurrence to my general conceptions of the world. What makes me suspect that people really do exaggerate a little when they report marvels (it is so hard to astonish!) is not the apparent frequency of such events, but the comparative scarcity of gibbering sceptics.

VI

I DON'T THINK the social atmosphere was always as unfavourable
to good talk as it is at present. People used to be more patient;
dread of the monologue or of prolonged discussion was not
so intense; the ban upon the longer story was less severe. I can
hardly doubt that some of the famous talkers of the past, like
Coleridge, Carlyle or Oscar Wilde, would still dominate their
company, but I am less certain that they would be so much
admired and encouraged.

The fame of talkers, alas, is as unsubstantial as the fame of
actors. The recorded scraps of old discourse give us little sense
of the brilliance of conversation in the past—as little as the
specimens which travellers bring home suggest the fertility and
wonder of distant lands.

The tradition of Coleridge's amazing and unique powers of
discourse is part of the history of English Literature. His talk
has been described by many contemporaries. Carlyle's description, too well known to quote, in the *Life of Sterling*, is the most
famous. But we must remember that this is a description of his
talk in Highgate days, when a preaching tone had crept into his
voice, and he was less inspired and more diffuse than when in
his youth he astounded Hazlitt and De Quincey. In youth and
middle-age talk had been his refuge from disappointment,
bewilderment, and shame. In the glow of it, in the wonder he
excited, he could forget that he was a gigantic failure (how
absurd this verdict sounds now!) in his eyes, and in those of all
who loved him. But under the care of the good Gillmans he had
become more or less reconciled to his own nature, while his
allowance of opium had been restricted to an amount which
gave exhilaration and relief, but did not incapacitate. A modern
critic is right when he says 'he had been so ecstatic a talker
because he was in flight from a fiend, and when the fiend ceased
to pursue him he tended to lapse into a sententious amble.'

Carlyle when he visited Highgate had too many undelivered
lay sermons in him to find satisfaction as a passive bucket to be

pumped into. But though he did not admire, he wondered at 'those sunny domes, those caves of ice' which Coleridge built in air. 'Glorious islets, too,' he says, 'I have seen rise out of the haze; but they were few and soon swallowed in the general element again. Balmy, sunny islets, islets of the blest and intelligible.'

There is a half-forgotten, anonymous little book called *Conversations at Cambridge*. The author was an old school-fellow of Coleridge, C. V. Le Grice, who is mentioned by Lamb in that essay on Christ's Hospital which contains a much more sympathetic description than Carlyle's of Coleridge's extraordinary gift. In the summer of 1833, a year before his death, Coleridge paid a visit to Cambridge. In 1793, distracted by debt and love, he had run away from Cambridge and enlisted in a dragoon regiment. 'My emotions,' he wrote, 'on revisiting the University on this occasion were at first overwhelming. I could not speak for an hour; yet my feelings were, upon the whole, pleasurable and I have not passed, of late years at least, three days of such great enjoyment and healthful excitement of mind and body.' He was put up in Trinity. He did not rise till the afternoon, when he held a crowded levee, and he seems to have talked all night.

It is this talk which Le Grice endeavours to recapture. Unlike Carlyle, he cannot imagine anyone wishing 'to punctuate by a single question that rich musical discourse.' Although he took notes while the poet's voice was still in his ears, it is seldom we can hear that voice. Sometimes, however, we do: 'How the heart opens at the magic name of Milton! Yet who shall, in our day, hang another garland on his tomb!' I fancy that is verbatim. It has Coleridge's soaring effectiveness. But when the reporter goes on, recording the excellent criticism which follows, the words have no longer a spoken quality, only a stately tameness. It is almost in every case only in the exordium we hear the living voice: 'And why should I not call Taylor a poet? Is not 'Holy Living and Dying' a sacred and didactic poem in almost as wide a sense as the 'Commedia' of Dante? What bard of

ancient and modern times has surpassed, in richness of language, in fertility of fancy, in majesty of sentiment, in grace of
imagery, this Spenser of English prose?'

The great crystal has begun to swing. He divagates; he quotes
at a length, which attests the possession of astonishing memory,
prose passages equal to 'the sublimest poetry,' adding: 'How
pleasant it would be to go on thus. if my memory would enable
me, gathering choice specimens of sublimity, pathos, and picturesque truth; collecting the precious stones of which his
charms are strung; for even his ornaments are never chosen for
their lustre alone; and in the most gorgeous festivals and riotous
enjoyments of his imagination, a Hand is perceived writing on
the wall. Never did a soldier of the Holy Cross issue forth in a
more gorgeous equipment to fight for the Sepulchre of Christ.
But the resplendent sword is of celestial temper, and that costly
armour was mighty against the dart of the enemy as any coat of
mail; it protected while it shone.' You must imagine the face
of the speaker, rapt, radiant, moist—his eyes 'sending out great
signals.' 'I am glad,' wrote that matter-of-fact Miss Martineau,
'to have seen his weird face and heard his dreamy voice; and my
notion of possession, prophecy—of involuntary speech for
involuntary brain-action has been clearer ever since.' Thus
Coleridge talked. To talk like that now would be like singing
at dinner.

VII

CARLYLE'S TALK, though utterly different from that of Coleridge,
must have been as remarkable. He, too, was an oratorical talker,
but he excelled particularly in vehement denunciation, in fantastic and vivid bluster. There were sardonic surprises in it.
I heard George Meredith imitate him once; it was a *crescendo* of
picturesque curses which ended in a shout of laughter, laughter
which subsided gradually into a wistful stillness, while Carlyle
would slowly rub his hands up and down his shins and sigh,
'Ah, weel, ah, weel.' His chief intellectual fault as a talker seems
to have been that, according to him, no one could be actively

interested in the progress of the species without being off his balance and in need of tenderness from his friends. He would speak of himself as though he were all his life compelled to the dismal necessity of ransacking the graves of the dead in order to find some poor spangle, still untarnished, of nobility in human nature. This must have been tiresome in the long run. 'You wondered at last,' Henry James, Senior, said of him, 'how any mere mortal got legitimately endowed with a commiseration so divine for the inferior race of man.' There was clearly more of the play-actor in his talk than there was in Coleridge's. But what a splendid performance it must have been! And how amusing! What gibes he flung about him; now at the Quaker orator, Bright—'pugnacious, cock-nosed John'; now at Ruskin—'a beautiful bottle of soda water'; now at Mill, the Saint of Rationalism—'saw-dust up to the mast-head.' A humorist, you see, in the guise of a Jeremiah! There were often stirring scenes in the little sitting-room in Cheyne Row; perhaps a merciless mellay if a belligerent with sturdy opinions of his own dropped in. At the bare mention of certain topics Mrs Carlyle would nudge a sympathetic neighbour and whisper in dread, 'Now for the deluge.' Down sure enough it would come, hot and heavy for an hour or more. But nothing exasperated Carlyle so much as the reverential readers who offered devout and grateful homage. Such adorers reminded him too intimately of the essentially histrionic and humoristic nature of his genius beneath its apocalyptic cloak: their simplicity was an insult. They were intolerable bores; and, as a lighthouse-keeper finds lying, after a storm, upon the platform round the lamp, birds which have dashed themselves against it, so, he used to say, did he expect to find every morning the bodies of several dead Americans on his doorstep. Even if his fame as a talker had not survived, even if his spoken phrases were not still flying from mouth to mouth, from his style alone, from its vehemence and its vividness, posterity would have guessed that Carlyle must have been a glorious converser. His talk must have been inferior only to his best prose.

VIII

WITH REGARD to Wilde's talk, tradition is unanimous: it was more
surprising than his writing. I have often interrogated those who
heard him. Wilfred Blunt and Max Beerbohm both told me that,
in their experience of talkers, it was a case of 'Oscar' first and the
rest nowhere. The variety of his range, too, was astonishing. He
excelled in nonsense, in repartee, in description, in narration, in
sentiment, and he excelled too in that general kind of talk,
ranging over biography and history, in which for the most part
men like Lord Morley, with well-stored minds and with experience in affairs, are easily first. Wilde was also an exceedingly
amiable talker, uncompetitive, and immensely appreciative of
other people's contributions. That remarkable biography, *The
Life of Oscar Wilde* by Frank Harris, is full of convincing records
of his talk. You will find in a little book by Laurence Housman
Echo de Paris, *A Study from Life*, an account of a restaurant conversation which took place after Wilde's release from prison.
Twenty-four years is a long time to carry talk in one's head, even
Oscar Wilde's; but it can be done, and probably Mr Housman
took notes at the time. The prelude to the luncheon is characteristic. Oscar Wilde is a little late; he enters with deliberate
ironical reference to his imprisonment. 'But what are two
minutes in three years of a disintegrated lifetime ? It is almost
three years, is it not, since we missed seeing each other ?' There
is a slightly uncomfortable pause, when, as it were a minstrel
throwing back his cloak to pluck a few chords upon his instrument, the famous talker begins. What he says is not in substance
very remarkable. It is the grace, finish, and flexibility of the
performance that delights. The suggestion which he makes that
Carlyle lost his chance of producing a permanent work of art
greater than his *French Revolution* by choosing Frederick the
Great instead of Napoleon is interesting; also the suggestion
that Carlyle did so because he worshipped success: 'I have come
to see that St Helena is, for a world which follows Caesar and not
Christ, the greatest place on earth next to Calvary.' Then the

significance of failure (he is thinking of himself) becomes the main theme of his discourse; but the charm and, I am sure, the verisimilitude lie in the skill with which the talker keeps modulating into a lighter key and out of it again, backwards and forwards. I feel sure that it was this faculty which made Oscar Wilde's conversation such an astonishing performance. I know no living talkers who equal this, or who seem to take conversation seriously as an art. Good talkers nowadays are proud of taking no trouble. It is the fashion of sincerity.

The two talkers I have known in recent times whose sentences would probably read best if written down are Bernard Shaw and Sir Edmund Gosse. The only talker I have heard who will launch the high poetic phrase (in conversation) is Yeats. He will say that 'the music of Heaven is full of the clashing of swords' without seeming conscious that others might conclude that he was talking for effect. I like that myself. And even if he were talking for effect, I should, for my part, only be the more grateful for a fine ambitious phrase. When I meet those remarkable people whose company is coveted, I often wish that they would show off a little more.